The Abdication of King Edward VIII

The Abdication

of

King Edward VIII

BY

LORD BEAVERBROOK

EDITED BY

A. J. P. TAYLOR

UNT 240

Atheneum, New York
1966

Illustrations

Foreword

LORD BEAVERBROOK completed this book on the abdication of King Edward VIII in 1958. He had been interested in the subject for a long time. He supplied much material on it to other writers, including the Duke of Windsor, and in 1952 was stimulated by the last volume of *The History of the Times* into delivering a broadcast talk, pillorying Geoffrey Dawson. He followed this by preparing a glossy pamphlet which vindicated his broadcast against the critics. The pamphlet was not published. Instead Beaverbrook set to work on a full narrative of his own part in the King's Affair. By 1958 the final corrections had been made and the necessary permissions to use unpublished letters had been secured. All that remained was to devise chapter-headings and an effective title for the book itself—always with Beaverbrook the last, and in some ways the most difficult, part of his literary undertakings. Then Beaverbrook laid the book aside and never returned to it.

We can only speculate on the reasons for this. Beaverbrook was always tempted to go off on new enterprises, and he did so now. He worked on his early reminiscences and on the lives of two friends, R. B. Bennett and Sir James Dunn.[1] Also the Abdication book may have seemed rather short to come out on its own. In any case, Beaverbrook had another use for it. He had doubted his gifts as a historian.[2] The

---

[1] The life of Bennett was published as *Friends* (1959), and that of Dunn as *Courage* (1961).

[2] Hence he always published his books in relatively small editions, to prevent their being remaindered.

success of *Men and Power* surprised and encouraged him. He resolved to write a large work on *The Age of Baldwin*, in which he would at last triumph over his old antagonist. Little of this was accomplished. The introductory chapters swelled into a book and came out in 1963 as *The Decline and Fall of Lloyd George*. Thereafter was to follow a detailed account of the General Strike and of Beaverbrook's crusade for Empire Free Trade. The Abdication would provide the final section. These projects were not fulfilled. *The Age of Baldwin* was never written, and only the Abdication remains to show what we have lost.

The book, as it stands, is rather short. But it is Beaverbrook at his most sparkling, and it seems to me desirable to publish it, particularly as he himself had approved it. For one thing, it illuminates his method of writing and so enables scholars to estimate how far his other books are reliable. The documents which he derived from others have of course been scrupulously copied, though I think Beaverbrook sometimes put on the reminiscences of others a stronger interpretation than they could carry. The main evidence however comes from Beaverbrook himself, and it is clear that this rested almost solely on his memory. In *Politicians and the War*, he implies, though he does not assert, that the detailed narrative comes from a contemporary diary.[1] I do not believe that Beaverbrook ever kept a diary in his life. What he had was an engagement book, and he built up his narrative from this. 3 December is a good example. The engagement book reads baldly: 12.15 Lord Brownlow. 2.30 Sir W. Layton. 4.15 Lord Rothermere. Mr. Winston Churchill. 9.45 Mr. Allen. *Dinner*. Mr. Bracken, Mr. Bevan. Later this was expanded, partly from memory, and became:

> Lord Beaverbrook sees Mr. Churchill, Lord Rother-
> mere, Sir Walter Layton, and Mr. J. S. Elias; telephones
> the King at Fort Belvedere, and holds a conference at

[1] Thus (Vol. II, p. 144), 'I continue the narrative in diary form'.

8

Stornoway House with Mr. Walter Monckton, Mr. Allen, and Lord Brownlow. Later Mr. Churchill visits Lord Beaverbrook at Stornoway House and they make suggestions to Mr. Allen regarding proposed broadcast speech by the King.

As well, there are innumerable fragments dictated to secretaries or scribbled by Beaverbrook on scraps of paper. Many of these record remarks which he or others made at dinner. One, not used in the book, reads:

> Attlee.
> Disproves my Rule Don't Trust to Luck.

Another was a reminder: 'Rewrite Introduction and at speed', meaning that the Introduction should be given its present lively form. The engagement book and the notes started Beaverbrook's mind working, and his memory did the rest. Anyone who challenged him, even in extreme old age, will know that his memory was formidably accurate. It was memory all the same.

These personal recollections are welcome in themselves. They also provide, I think, some useful new information for historians. Beaverbrook explains his own position. He was not at this time, as he subsequently became, a close friend of the king's.[1] He did not share Churchill's romantic attachment to the Monarchy. At most, as a believer in Empire, he resented Baldwin's exploitation of alleged feeling in the Dominions. Of course he was pleased to be at the centre of events and delighted to work against Baldwin. His principal motive was one rarely credited to him and which yet was perhaps the strongest in his life. It was charity, the desire to help a human being in distress, particularly a human being harassed by the established order. Beaverbrook has been well called 'a foul-weather friend'; never more so than with King Edward VIII during this crisis.

[1] The first letter from the Duke of Windsor to Beaverbrook beginning 'My dear Max' is dated 15 August 1941.

The book goes far to explain a number of points in the affair which have not been clear before. Thus it puts the question of the intervention against Mrs. Simpson's decree *nisi* in a new light. It has sometimes been conjectured that the threat of this intervention was among the factors which led the King to abdicate. The truth seems the opposite. The law officers, and Sir John Simon also, took the view that the King could prevent any intervention so long as he remained on the throne, simply by ordering his servant, the King's Proctor, not to intervene. The Government could not give any such order and therefore could not guarantee what would happen once the King had abdicated. However, for reasons unknown, the King's Proctor did not in fact intervene.

The question of the morganatic marriage is of more importance. It is clear, as Beaverbrook realized, that from the moment the King proposed this, he put himself at the Government's mercy. He was now asking them for something, whereas previously they had been asking him. It was not Edward's idea. His original proposal was 'No marriage, No Coronation'—surely a more effective weapon. Why then did the King persist in the idea of a morganatic marriage when Beaverbrook and others warned him against it? The question can now be answered. The person who insisted on morganatic marriage, once it was proposed, was Mrs. Simpson herself. Hence the King had to persist in his turn. He could not accept Churchill's advice to reject the Government's interference into his private life. Morganatic marriage or abdication were the only alternatives, if he wished to marry Mrs. Simpson. She was much abused at the time. Yet she insisted on morganatic marriage, when objections were raised against her becoming Queen; and she urgently offered to withdraw altogether if the King would remain on the throne. Her generosity and unselfishness can now receive belated tribute. It was thanks to Mrs. Simpson, not to Baldwin, that the affair had so smooth an ending.

10

One part of this story looks forward to the future, to the history of the *Second World War*, which Beaverbrook also projected. The crisis brought Churchill and Beaverbrook together. Though they had been friends for many years, they rarely agreed on political matters. During the First World War and after it, Churchill distrusted the influence of Press Lords—Beaverbrook's almost as much as Northcliffe's. Later Churchill, as a convinced Free Trader, had no sympathy with Beaverbrook's campaign for Empire Free Trade. Beaverbrook, on his side, was not much moved by Churchill's campaign against constitutional concessions to India. Nor did they agree on foreign affairs. By 1936, Churchill was eager for collective security. Beaverbrook, though demanding rearmament, favoured isolation and an alliance with the United States. Once Baldwin had gone, Beaverbrook was on good terms with Neville Chamberlain. Nevertheless the Abdication forged a new intimacy between Churchill and Beaverbrook. In 1940 Churchill turned to Beaverbrook and found in him once more a foul-weather friend.

The editorial work in preparing this book for publication has been light. It has been made even lighter by the skilled co-operation of Miss R. C. Brooks, Lord Beaverbrook's secretary. Between us, we have checked the quotations and occasionally altered sentences made inappropriate by the passage of time. There are some mistakes which I should have pointed out to Lord Beaverbrook if he had shown the book to me in his lifetime. I doubt whether he would have accepted all my corrections. Now that he cannot stop me, I have put them into editorial footnotes. I hope I have done a good work for his memory.

A. J. P. Taylor

11

Introduction

THIS IS not a story of love and sacrifice, although love and sacrifice are its background. It is a political narrative of the events which led to a change in the succession to the throne.

It is told, not as an historical account of these events, but rather in the form of material for future historians. It is part of a series of books on politics and politicians under the general title *The Age of Baldwin*.

The King wanted to stay. He also wanted to marry.

The Archbishop did not want either the King or the marriage.

Baldwin, the Prime Minister, did not want King Edward and did not care about the marriage one way or the other.

The movement to deprive King Edward VIII of his royal inheritance was launched at the outset of his reign, before he had declared his love for Mrs. Simpson.

Instances of this early hostility, which swiftly grew as the days passed, can be multiplied:

(1) At the Accession Council held at St. James's Palace Attlee had a conversation with Baldwin[1]: 'I remember Baldwin expressing to me his anxiety for the future and his doubts as to whether the new King would stay the course.'

(2) Sir Samuel Hoare (later Lord Templewood) writes, 'Two of the new King's intimate advisers had told Baldwin after the funeral (of King George V) that the King had made up his mind to marry Mrs. Simpson.'

---

[1] Attlee: *As It Happened*, p. 85.

13

He refers to 'the trouble that had been brewing' and says that Baldwin's delay in acting was partly 'because he felt that his intervention might be resented by the public'.[1]

(3) In Lockhart's biography of Archbishop Lang there is mention of a long and intimate talk which the Archbishop had on the subject with King George V, 'whose closing days were clouded with anxiety for the future'.[2]

The Archbishop[3] wished to rid himself of his monarch because he was not a faithful and attentive son of the Church, and furthermore was drifting away from the Establishment. He would not go to church and he would go to night clubs.

Baldwin did not believe in the capabilities of His Majesty for the art of kingship and resented his independence of the politicians and his addiction to declaring himself on political issues without consultation with his constitutional advisers. Besides, they had not made friends when travelling together in Canada in 1927.

Members of the aristocracy wished to destroy the King. They deplored his liking for the company of married women and in particular Mrs. Simpson. They disliked his neglect of their circles with abhorrence for his addiction to what they called 'Café Society'—they declared that Buckingham Palace was drifting into the status of an American night-club.

But Baldwin had also another motive. He sought to bring about the restoration of his own political power and popu-

[1] Templewood: *Nine Troubled Years*, p. 215.
[2] Lockhart: *Cosmo Gordon Lang*, p. 396.
[3] The Archbishop's importance in public life is not readily understood, though recognized in official circles. He ranks next to the Royal Family and takes precedence over the Prime Minister. A curious survival of medieval forms of government, this Prelate is neither hereditary nor elected. He is nominated by the Prime Minister of the day. He sits in the House of Lords and gives out his opinions freely and without any other restraint than his clerical office.

larity. At that stage in his career, he had been a good deal damaged in public life by events connected with rearmament. He was believed by many to have behaved with cynicism and dishonesty.

By concealing from the public the need for heavier rearmament he had won an election—and had then admitted the deception.[1] On the eve of the Abdication, therefore, Baldwin needed political rehabilitation.

His political foresight, which was considerable, pictured the situation as a struggle between Parliament and King. On that wicket (as he would have said) Parliament was sure to win.

If necessary, he could make it appear that this was a battle of the people against the almost autocratic authority of a King who meant to have his own way.

There was, however, a skeleton at Baldwin's feast: What if he should lose his command over Parliament?

To hold the House he had to square the Socialists and the Liberals. As the narrative will show, this was effectively done.

But there was still the danger that Churchill, the King's champion, might be called to office, gathering followers from every side. Aneurin Bevan, the Socialist member, for instance, would have been ready to support the King.

A development of this kind would have made it impossible for the battle to be fought on the terms that Baldwin wished: People against Authority.

In the event, this danger to Baldwin's plan was averted. He did keep Churchill out and he did hold Parliament.

The King could have been saved from either the loss of his crown or his wife—or both. But no attempt was made to do so by the heads of Church or State.

The King was himself not without sin. He bears a share of the responsibility for what happened.

He was too unbending in his demands on the issue. He had

[1] [This version is not now accepted by historians.—Ed.]

a plan that he and Mrs. Simpson should be married before the Coronation.

He was content to have it either way: either she should sit on a throne in the Abbey as his Queen or in the stalls as his morganatic wife.

But, in the end, his attitude was brittle rather than rigid.

The Abdication crisis took place at a time when Europe was in a state of political disorder, with disruption impending. This grave problem was overshadowed in the public mind by the situation developing in Buckingham Palace.

People in Britain have always been interested in the doings of the squire and his family. That is their traditional attitude. The doings of the Royal family, which is the head of the squirearchy, come first in this universal appeal.

Our people were absorbed in them at a time when they should instead have given thought to the question, how could war be avoided.

They looked upon Stalin as a savage living in a cold country without the benefit of Church and incapable of any large or effective power beyond his own borders.

They thought of Hitler as a political phenomenon who would soon pass into oblivion.

The interest of the nation was centred on the cruise of the yacht *Nahlin* and an unknown American lady named Mrs. Simpson.

It is necessary then to set the crisis against the conditions prevailing in Europe in 1936. These are briefly described in the pages that follow, with the general conviction that had Britain devoted as much energy to wise and constructive policies of Empire as to driving King Edward from his inheritance then we might have been saved from the terrible struggle that lay three years ahead.

There is need for a study of the crisis by students of politics and constitutional issues. For what was done once, can be done again.

The Abdication of 1936 set a precedent which might be

16

followed in similar circumstances under a different political leadership and with catastrophic results.

The events of that year should therefore be carefully examined and long reflected on.

The Abdication came as a great shock to the nation and the constitutional system. Without doubt, the throne trembled.

But, during the reign of George VI, the monarchy withstood the blow. Many forces worked together to bring steadiness and recovery. One of them was his popular Queen, fortunately from a sound and strong Scottish family, not a foreign royalty. Churchill, the protagonist of King Edward, became a loyal, devoted and worldly-wise first Minister of the Crown.

So the damage was repaired and confidence in the monarchy has been restored.

I

AT THE outset of the new King's reign, I attended the swearing-in service at St. James's Palace. It was not my habit to attend official functions; indeed I avoided them. But on this occasion I was eager to pay homage to King Edward. A new reign, with a young and independent-minded sovereign, excited my imagination. I had high hopes and great expectations. I believed that Edward VIII would set a fresh tone and give a colourful leadership in the country.[1]

And so I struggled into the uniform of a Privy Councillor to be present at his investiture. It was the second time I had worn the uniform in twenty years, and it was a tight fit.

I knew King Edward slightly. I had been to dine with him at St. James's Palace on one occasion when J. H. Thomas, the Socialist Minister, was there. I took a minor part in the conversation. The Prince and Thomas appeared to be playing a game of verbal tennis. The scoring was fairly even, and I was content to watch the volley. The talk turned mainly on unemployment.

Later, he dined with me at Stornoway House.[2] The guests were made up of my own group of friends and had not been gathered for the purpose of entertaining the Prince of Wales. Dean Inge and his wife were among them. He was a man I

[1] I expressed these views in a letter to my old friend Joseph M. Patterson of the New York *Daily News*. See Appendix D (i).

[2] Stornoway House fronted Green Park. It was destroyed by a land mine in 1940 and the building so shattered as to be beyond repair. Happily the contents of the wine cellar escaped damage—a very real blessing in the days of short supply. The house has been reconstructed as an office building.

19

greatly admired, and for whom I cherished a warm affection.

The night was particularly foggy, and the Prince set out to walk to the Palace alone. I insisted on accompanying him.

The faith and confidence in the new reign, which I shared with the great majority of the British people, were not held by the Prime Minister and the Archbishop of Canterbury.[1] The attitude of the Prince towards religion had created distrust in the minds of the Church of England leaders. The Archbishop had shared the family confidences and anxieties of King George V, and if he hoped for the best, he also feared (and expected) the worst.[2]

There was also some discord and resentment in the political field. There were two schools of thought in the Socialist Party in 1936. One school was totally pacifist. The other school was not exactly pacifist but it believed in Peace Without Tears, through the influence and authority of the League of Nations, and no militarism. In 1935 the Prince of Wales, as he then was, had publicly declared his disbelief in Pacifism.[3] His scepticism as to the efficacy of the League of Nations was almost equally undisguised, and gave offence to both parties.

He gave further offence by his open advocacy of a policy of friendship with Germany. In June 1935 he addressed the British Legion and proposed that a deputation of ex-Servicemen should go to Germany on a mission of reconciliation. It was a breach of constitutional usage for the Prince of Wales to seek to further any controversial policy in public, and the policy of Anglo-German friendship ran contrary to the policy of the Foreign Office at that time.[4]

[1] The Archbishop was described by a distinguished ecclesiastic as 'a renegade Presbyterian'.

[2] See J. G. Lockhart: *Cosmo Gordon Lang*, p. 398.

[3] In a speech at Berkhamsted School in 1935 he attacked the L.C.C. for forbidding the use even of wooden guns by the O.T.C.s in the schools under L.C.C. control.

[4] In July of the same year he was guest of honour at the German Embassy. No member of the Royal Family had been at the Embassy since 1914.

20

He made enemies among politicians by his habit of discussing them in free and unflattering terms with no regard as to who might be listening. On the other hand, he had a genuine respect for the two most eminent politicians of the day, David Lloyd George and Winston Churchill. It happened that both were abroad when George V died. Churchill had just presented Lloyd George with one of his pictures, which was most gratefully received.

'Your picture is a real joy,' Lloyd George wrote. 'I have never professed to be an art critic but I know when a picture gives me a thrill which increases every time I see it. That is certainly my experience with yours. I was so delighted with it that, although I had already taken my tickets for the West Indies, I was half persuaded to cancel them and return to that dream of colour which you so effectively depict.

'I am very grateful to you. I have fixed the picture in the new room where I now do all my work, and I am sure you will feel glad to know that it will cheer an old fellow who is a friend and admirer of your genius.[1]

'I am so glad you are coming to the private dinner organised by Ivor Nicholson to celebrate the completion of my labours.[2] When are you coming to see me here,[3] as you promised?

'God's in His Heaven and Baldwin is back in Downing Street.'

Lloyd George was fully in sympathy with the King's desire to get on friendly terms with Germany. Indeed, he went much further than the new King. He paid a visit to Germany in that year and had several meetings with Ribbentrop and with Hitler himself.[4] When he went to Berchtesgaden

[1] The painting of Marrakesh given by Churchill to Lloyd George is now hanging in the Art Gallery at Fredericton, New Brunswick, Canada.
[2] The 'Labours' were the Lloyd George Memoirs.
[3] Churt, Lloyd George's home in Surrey.
[4] The Duke of Windsor, accompanied by the Duchess, visited Ribbentrop in Germany in 1937. His Royal Highness and the Duchess met Hitler in Berchtesgaden. The visit roused much criticism.

for a little tea-party Hitler presented him with his photograph. This gift roused in Lloyd George an even deeper emotion than the Churchill painting.

'One seemed to be witnessing an act of reconciliation between the two nations,' wrote a friend of Lloyd George who was present. Lloyd George got up to shake hands with the Führer and thank him for his gift. He asked if there would be any objection to his putting it on his desk along with the photographs of Foch, Clemenceau and other Allied leaders who had won the War against Germany. Hitler graciously said he had no objection, for there was no shame in losing a war, and the defeat of Germany had been brought about by one great statesman—'Yourself, Mr. Lloyd George.'

Lloyd George was greatly moved. He said he was proud to hear such compliments from the greatest German of the age, and added that it was an immense advantage for Europe to have strong men in charge of affairs. Refusing to be outdone in compliments, Hitler said that Lloyd George was the only statesman in Europe to understand his policies.[1]

When Lloyd George returned to England, he wrote an article for the *Daily Express*, giving an enthusiastic account of his experiences. He also gave interviews in the same strain, declaring that the Germans were the happiest people in the world. I was much interested in these opinions, but was far from agreeing with them. I wrote to Lloyd George on 6th October, 1936:

'I have been very interested in your German experiences and the viewpoints you brought back from that country. I went there too. But I hated so much the regimentation of opinion that I could not bear it.

'I was in Berlin at the opening of the Olympic Games. On that occasion privilege and class had a run, the like of which has not existed in this country since the aristocracy began to marry chorus girls.

[1] Lloyd George said that he supported Germany in 1936 because he feared the overthrow of Hitler would result in the rise of Stalin.

'However, this is only my point of view. I do not present it to you as an argument. On subjects of this kind there is no use arguing. Men's opinions are bound to differ.

'I think Baldwin will retire soon. And when Chamberlain comes to form his Government, he will demote Duff Cooper, who has been a dreadful failure at the War Office. He made a muddle of his recruiting for the Army.'[1]

My disagreement with Lloyd George was mild compared with Churchill's. At this time Churchill was using all his immense energy and his eloquence to bring the nation to a realization of the menace of German militarism that threatened them once again. Events have justified his warning, but at the time his voice was disregarded and he succeeded only in making himself unpopular.

But although he and Lloyd George were flatly opposed on this great issue,[2] they were both on terms of cordial friendship with the King and were entirely loyal.

Unfortunately both Lloyd George and Churchill were out of office, and both looked like being out for the rest of their lives. The Prime Minister, Mr. Stanley Baldwin, appeared to be strong and confident of himself. He, like the Archbishop

[1] [Beaverbrook's prophecy did not prove true. Duff Cooper was made First Lord of the Admiralty and so survived to become the hero of Munich.—Ed.]

[2] Although Churchill and Lloyd George were diametrically opposed in their German policies, each at least did have a policy which was clear-cut and comprehensible. It was not so with Baldwin. Faced with the revival of German militarism he could have followed one of two courses. If he had undertaken rapid and heavy rearmament he would have prevented war. But Baldwin did not take this course. Indeed, in the 1935 Election he gave public assurances that there would be no massive rearmament.

His other course was to form an alliance with U.S.A., and stand aloof from the European conflict. That was the policy I urged upon the Government and advocated in the *Daily Express*. In that event, Germany and Russia might have torn each other to pieces.

But Baldwin had no clear policy at all. When the German threat overshadowed everything else he drifted into an effort to defeat Mussolini—and drifted out again. For long periods he was totally silent on foreign affairs, while public anxiety grew and the danger of war increased with every hour.

23

of Canterbury, had a temperamental incompatibility with the King. The King found Baldwin something of a bore, and he suffered from his flow of unwanted information during a Canadian tour which they undertook together. It was not a happy start for the close relationship which must subsist between King and Prime Minister, but I could well understand the King's feelings.

In all my fifty years of political activity I have never known a character so complex as Stanley Baldwin. Under a surface air of geniality he was a thoroughly good hater. For example, he hated Lloyd George—both hated and feared him. He frequently asserted that Lloyd George was a spent force, but in his heart he knew better and dreaded the devastating effect of Lloyd George's invective.

He also hated me, most intensely. The reason for this hatred was curious and enlightening. We had been friendly for a good many years and, indeed, I had secured for him his first political promotion as Joint Financial Secretary to the Treasury under Bonar Law. That was in the first World War. We made common cause in 1922 when Lloyd George was overthrown, but we did not have any intimate contact.[1]

His anger was unrestrained when I attacked him in 1923 vehemently over his settlement of the American Loan,[2] and

[1] Lloyd George was overthrown at the Carlton Club meeting. Austen Chamberlain was leader of the Tories at the time, and he was opposed by Bonar Law. The defeat of Chamberlain ended the Coalition. Bonar Law formed a purely Tory Government. Baldwin became Chancellor of the Exchequer.

[2] During the first World War we borrowed large sums from U.S.A. and lent even more to our Allies. Bonar Law maintained that the only just settlement was an all-round settlement, our borrowings being offset by our lendings. I strongly supported the Bonar Law contention. A one-sided settlement with U.S.A. would leave us obliged to repay all we had borrowed, with no prospect of getting back what we had lent. As Bonar Law's Chancellor of the Exchequer, Baldwin went to Washington with Montagu Norman to discuss the American Debt. He sent back by wire proposals the Americans had made for a one-sided settlement. Bonar Law rejected the proposals and recalled him for consultations, but on arriving at Southampton Baldwin told reporters that the terms offered by the Americans were the best that could be expected. Thus, before he had

24

matters were not improved by the tittle tattle of his friends who took care to tell him of every jibe I made against him. He returned these jibes with interest, and made a number of really amusing sallies at my expense. His anger against me was much increased by my hostile attitude during the Election of 1923.[1] The *Observer*, the *Morning Post* and the *Yorkshire Post* all declared that I was responsible for his defeat on that occasion. I held no such opinion. But the verdict of these newspapers was not calculated to make him love me the more.

In the election of 1924 I supported Baldwin, but we did not reach any understanding. We made an agreement to work together in 1931 but we swiftly faced a rupture of our relations; and his hatred and distrust of me became a positive obsession.[2]

Baldwin was a man of pretences. When he had friends in his library, he would walk round picking volumes from the shelves and reading out passages, with appropriate comments.

discussed the matter with his chief, he had recommended that the American terms should be accepted, and Bonar Law was left with the alternatives of agreeing the terms or repudiating his own Chancellor and bringing down his Government. Baldwin had made an immense and disastrous blunder, and I attacked him fiercely for it. The Cabinet decided that there was nothing to be done but accept the American terms. But the terms proved so onerous that they had subsequently to be repudiated.

[1] I refused to support Baldwin in 1923 because he had rejected my plea for Imperial Preference and insisted on going to the country on an issue of insular protection.

[2] For many years our relationship was very much a matter of up and down. In 1929 when he was out of office he paid me a compliment at a great Albert Hall meeting. He said, 'We owe a debt of gratitude to one not always a supporter of our party, Lord Beaverbrook, for bringing before the country once more the idea—of which we have heard too little in recent years—of a United Empire. I pay tribute to his courage—rare in one of his profession—in offering a subject he believes in to criticism in its proper place—the Houses of Parliament.'

But it was down in 1932 when he was in Downing Street. As Leader of the Party, he was invited to unveil a memorial portrait of Bonar Law at the Constitutional Club. He refused to go unless he was given an assurance that I would not be allowed to take part. To save the organizers embarrassment, I withdrew my acceptance of their invitation.

This gave a pleasant impression of culture, though I doubt if he was really a deeply-read man. But he had another use for his library. He would frequently retire there to make a careful study of State papers, or so he would explain. But when he had safely locked the door, he would stretch himself in an arm-chair by the fire with a detective story until he fell peacefully asleep. I sometimes suspected that even his famous pipe was more of a pose than a pleasure. Certainly I have seen him take it from his mouth with a wry expression which suggested that he was far from enjoying his smoke.

He was a thoroughly lazy man, but he was capable of immense energy when his own position was threatened. Whenever he was in danger he became a cool, determined, relentless and far-sighted adversary. He showed all the wisdom of the serpent. In the crisis of the King he was to do more. He was to show the serpent's venom as well.

Baldwin was a man of few friends. His intimates included Geoffrey Dawson of *The Times*, J. C. C. Davidson (now Lord Davidson), his ever faithful acolyte, and Montagu Norman of the Bank of England. None of his Cabinet colleagues was really close to him. Indeed, most of them regarded him with some suspicion. They believed that they could not rely on his loyalty.

This was the man who was to challenge the King and to thrust him off the Throne.

There were many minor disturbances between the Monarch and his Government. The hostility of the Administration against Italy and the imposition of sanctions, following the Italian invasion of Abyssinia, did not meet with support from Buckingham Palace.[1]

When the Negus, in flight from the Italians, sought sanctuary in England, Anthony Eden, Foreign Secretary, asked the King to receive the fallen ruler. The King refused.[2] His opposition to the League of Nations[3] also gave offence to several Ministers.

[1] *A King's Story*, p. 297. [2] *A King's Story*, p. 296. [3] *A King's Story*, p. 277.

The inner circles were distressed and even dismayed by the freedom of Edward VIII's opinions openly spoken on many political issues, and usually hostile to the Administration. Still there was no public criticism of the King's attitude. All seemed to be set fair.[1]

The threat to the Throne was to come from quite another source. While the popularity of the King was unchallenged and appeared to be unchallengeable, there were rumours in Fleet Street.

These were strengthened by a photograph of a small group at a window of Saint James's Palace watching a ceremonial parade. It was an intimate gathering of the King's close friends, but there was a woman among them whose face was unfamiliar. Who was this unknown lady? Inquiries were at once set on foot and her identity was promptly discovered.

She was Mrs. Simpson.

[1] During the King's reign, J. H. Thomas had been compelled to resign following the disclosure of a Budget leakage. In the King's recollection, he showed Thomas a great deal of sympathy during their parting interview when Thomas surrendered his seals of office. But Thomas's recollection was different. He said that the King first expressed sympathy and then 'scragged' him, because of the doubtful company Thomas had been keeping. The Archbishop subsequently made the same charge against the King.

II

THE PEOPLE of Britain were soon to hear much more of
Mrs. Simpson. In the Court Circular[1] it was announced that
Mr. and Mrs. Simpson had dined as guests of the King in a
company which also included Mr. and Mrs. Baldwin. Her
name appeared again in the Court Circular as guest at a
second dinner, but without her husband.

In the second week in August, the King went on a holiday
cruise in the Mediterranean in the chartered yacht *Nahlin*.[2]
The Press published the names of the guests. Mrs. Simpson
was among them. Mr. Simpson was not.[3] There were photographs of the King and Mrs. Simpson in the newspapers.

Shortly after the King's return to England he went to
Balmoral with a few personal friends. Again Mrs. Simpson
was among them, and again Mr. Simpson was not.

Although no word of comment had appeared in the British
Press, rumour was rife among the people. The American

[1] The Court Circular is issued daily from wherever the King is officially
in residence. It mentions his official engagements and the visitors he has
received.

[2] The *Nahlin* was the property of Lady Yule, the immensely wealthy
widow of the eccentric multi-millionaire Sir David Yule who began life
in Scotland as a poor boy and ended as the richest man of business in
India.

[3] The following guests were listed in the Press: Mrs. Ernest Simpson;
Duff Cooper and Lady Diana Cooper; Lord and Lady Brownlow; Lord
Dudley; Lord and Lady Louis Mountbatten; Mrs. Evelyn Fitzgerald;
Lady Cunard; Archie Compston, golfer; Herman and Katherine Rogers
(American friends of Mrs. Simpson); Major Sir John Aird—King's
equerry; Major Humphrey Butler—equerry to the Duke of Kent, and
Mrs. Butler; Sir Godfrey Thomas—private secretary; Commander Colin
Buist—King's equerry, and Mrs. Buist.

Press suffered from no inhibitions and printed the most sensational stories. The Hearst newspapers even published a statement with some apparent authority behind it, that the King intended to marry Mrs. Simpson.[1] The British Press made no reference to this startling declaration, but it could not be totally concealed from the British people. The word began to go round.

Until the middle of October, I myself knew no more about the affair than the general public. I had seen Mrs. Simpson, but only once and for a fleeting moment at a party given at Wimborne House. I knew, of course, about the American publicity, and the *Evening Standard* had been under pressure to publish 'revelations' offered by interested parties who wanted to bring the King's private friendship into public view. These offers were ignored. But the case was altered when the *Evening Standard* learned in the ordinary way of news gathering that Mrs. Simpson's divorce suit would be heard at Ipswich on 27th October. This news reached the newspaper about a fortnight before the hearing. It is, of course, common practice to publish advance intimation of a divorce action, if public interest warrants it. Judged by the ordinary standards of news value, publication was warranted in this instance. Mrs. Simpson's name was by this time familiar to the British public, and her friendship with the King was known. Her divorce undoubtedly was news.

Nevertheless the editor of the *Evening Standard*, Mr. Percy Cudlipp, consulted me on the advisability of publication. I advised in favour of it. After all, the King's name would not, and could not, be brought into a private action launched by one citizen against another. The King cannot be called to his own court.[2]

[1] Miss Marion Davies, friend of the late William Randolph Hearst, visited at Buckingham Palace. She has been credited with informing the *New York American* of the King's intention to marry Mrs. Simpson. The story appeared in that newspaper on 26th October, 1936.

[2] This immunity applies only to the King. Any other member of the Royal Family may be summoned to appear in Court. Edward the

But I was an old friend of Mr. Theodore Goddard, the distinguished solicitor who was acting for Mrs. Simpson, and I thought it advisable to telephone him and tell him what I meant to do. He at once asked me for an interview and I saw him that night. Mr. Goddard was understandably anxious to secure privacy for his client, but I was unconvinced by his representations and he left me without having received any assurance that publication would be withheld.

It was the failure of Mr. Goddard's mission that brought me for the first time into personal contact with the affair. It was on Tuesday, 13th October, exactly one week before he saw the Prime Minister, that the King telephoned me and asked me to see him at Buckingham Palace. When I asked him to fix the time of the appointment, he said in effect, 'name your own time', which led me to believe that he was exceedingly anxious for the interview. I was cursed with toothache and heavily engaged with my dentist during the next two days.[1]

On Friday, 16th October, I went to the Palace.

The King asked me to help in suppressing all advance news of the Simpson divorce, and in limiting publicity after the event. He stated his case calmly and with considerable cogency and force.

The reasons he gave for this wish were that Mrs. Simpson was ill, unhappy, and distressed by the thought of notoriety. Notoriety would attach to her only because she had been his guest on the *Nahlin* and at Balmoral. As the publicity would be due to her association with himself, he felt it his duty to protect her.

These reasons appeared satisfactory to me, and so I took part in a negotiation to confine the publication of the news

Seventh, when he was Prince of Wales, gave evidence in the celebrated Baccarat Case which caused a great deal of scandal at the time.

[1] [Beaverbrook saw Mr. Goddard at 6 p.m. on 12th October. There is no record in the engagement book of any visit by Beaverbrook to the dentist between 12th and 16th October. The book however contains this entry for 15th October: 5.30. Mr. Ernest Simpson.—Ed.]

"FIRST I GIVE YOU THE FACTS"—LORD BEAVERBROOK
FACES THE TELEVISION CAMERAS

MRS. WINFIELD SPENCER,
LATER MRS. SIMPSON, ON HER WEDDING DAY

LORD MOUNTBATTEN AND FRIENDS, 1935

THE KING AND HIS PARTY AT SALZBURG

MEDITERRANEAN
HOLIDAY
(left) BY THE SEASIDE
(below) IN THE SEA

MEDITERRANEAN HOLIDAY
(above) A LITTLE EXCURSION
(below) ANOTHER, IN ATHENS

AT BALMORAL

A HIGHLAND OCCASION

to a report of Mrs. Simpson's divorce, making no mention of her friendship with the King.

Mr. Walter Monckton, K.C., and Mr. Allen, both legal advisers to the King, came to see me. Mr. Monckton was Attorney-General to the Duchy of Cornwall, and Mr. Allen was the King's solicitor. In company with Mr. Monckton I visited Esmond Harmsworth. He was Chairman of the Newspaper Proprietors' Association. There and then, under his leadership, we arranged the plan of campaign. Most of the British newspapers consented without much difficulty to the policy of discretion. Sir Walter Layton of the *News Chronicle* hesitated, but I went to see him, and after consideration he took the same line as the other newspapers. The King sent him a letter of thanks for his co-operation.

I made representations to Mr. Alexander Ewing of the Outram Newspapers in Glasgow[1] and Mr. James Henderson of the *Belfast News-Letter*. They both agreed to limit publicity for the divorce story.

Ireland presented a different problem. To the great majority of the citizens of the Irish Free State, the British monarchy made no instinctive appeal. On the contrary, the monarchy stirred in them memories not unlike those stirred in Americans by the memory of the reign of George III. The intangible social pressures that were so effective in Great Britain had no efficacy at all for the majority in the Irish Free State. Nevertheless, I telephoned Dr. Lombard Murphy, owner of the *Irish Independent*.[2] He wrote on the 26th October, in the following terms:

'Subsequent to our telephone conversation to-day it occurred to me that probably the best way to ensure that the *Irish Press* does not splash the Simpson divorce case would be for you to get in touch with De Valera either

[1] The Outram Press owned the *Glasgow Herald*, the *Bulletin* and the Glasgow *Evening Times*.
[2] There were three newspapers of national circulation in Ireland: the *Irish Independent*, the *Irish Press* and the *Irish Times*.

31

directly or through Dulanty, the I.F.S. High Commissioner in London. I will not forget to ring up the Editor of the *Irish Times.*'

The case of the French Press was even more difficult. In one of the many telephone messages that the King sent me at that time, he drew my attention to an article in *Paris-Soir*, and asked me to approach that paper, and also the American newspapers. I spoke with M. Jean Prouvost of *Paris-Soir*, who replied in very cordial terms. He wrote on 28th October:

'You know what respectful esteem I have for your venerated Sovereign. Also, I only allowed the *Paris-Soir* to tell of the indignation of the English public at the indiscretions committed by the American press and radio on the project of the marriage of your Monarch, after having weighed all the terms of the article which was published yesterday, and giving, of course, the semi-official denial of the Court.

'I understand very well that such a subject is very delicate. I have therefore ordered our chief editors to abstain from mentioning it again in the future unless the requirements of the information compel me imperatively: *in which case I will telephone you beforehand.*'

I replied on 30th October:

'Very grateful thanks for your letter, which I have handed to the King. If you have occasion to telephone me about any further news that you think should be published, you will find me available at any time. Of course we do not want to limit the scope of your journalistic activities in the remotest degree. The sole purpose of the application to you is to escape, as far as possible, the publication of unjustifiable gossip concerning the King.'

While I was engaged in these activities directed to regulating newspaper publicity, I had no knowledge that marriage

was in the mind of the King.[1] He himself had given me no
hint of the matter, and, at the same time, I had been told by
Mrs. Simpson's solicitor, Mr. Theodore Goddard, that His
Majesty had no such intention. I repeated that assurance to
other newspaper proprietors. And I believed it.

Even if I had known that he did propose marriage, I
would still have done what I did. But the fact remains that I
did not know, although I was having conversations with the
King almost every day.

The divorce case was heard at Ipswich on 27th October.
It was duly reported in the Press without any sensationalism
and with no reference to the King. But there was a good deal
of unjustified comment in private on the fact that it was not
heard in London, where Mrs. Simpson was a resident. This
procedure was quite in order, for an Act of 1920 had made
it possible to have a divorce petition heard outside of London.[2] The comment was caused only because this provision
of the Act was not well known, and few people had
previously taken advantage of it.[3]

[1] The King made elaborate calculations. Mrs. Simpson's divorce would
not be completed until the end of April, 1937. Coronation had been fixed
for 10th May. It was the intention of His Majesty to marry Mrs. Simpson
in the first days of May. At the Coronation she would sit beside him on
the throne as Queen, or in the stalls as his morganatic wife.
'No marriage, no Coronation!' was his frequently repeated declaration,
taking the form of a dictum absolute and final and beyond appeal.
[2] See also the Goddard statement, Appendix C.
[3] Divorce in 1936 was a prolonged legal process. Trial was followed by
a 'decree *nisi*'. Then after six months, if there was no intervention by the
official known as the King's Proctor, the decree absolute was granted and
the marriage was at an end.

III

SHORTLY AFTER the divorce proceedings, I was asked to dine by Lord Brownlow,[1] to meet the King. The invitation was for Wednesday, 4th November, and I had another engagement. I hoped that I would hear no more of the matter, for I was shortly going to Canada.

By this time I was beginning to doubt the assurance of 'no marriage'. The King's attitude was so intense that it seemed to me impossible that it could be based on the issue of Mrs. Simpson's divorce publicity alone. As a newspaper proprietor I wanted to stand down from intimate consultations with the King and to regain my liberty of expression in my own newspapers.

However, Lord Brownlow asked me to name any other night, and I arranged the night following, Thursday, 5th November. The dinner was most interesting, for Mrs. Simpson was present, as well as the King.

She appeared to me to be a simple woman. She was plainly dressed and I was not attracted to her style of hairdressing.

---

[1] Lord Brownlow, whose home is at Belton, near Grantham, was the King's very intimate friend. He was Lord Lieutenant of Lincolnshire. When the King came to the Throne Lord Brownlow was appointed a non-political Lord in Waiting. The salary of six hundred pounds a year was not a consideration, for Lord Brownlow is a very wealthy Peer. The duties of the post could hardly be described as onerous. A Lord in Waiting has six weeks of duty in the course of the year. He represents the King at public functions and receives Cabinet Ministers, Ambassadors and other important persons who call on the King. He has the right to a free lunch every day of his period of duty. Lords in Waiting are prohibited from speaking against the Government or voting against it.

Her smile was kindly and pleasing, and her conversation was interspersed with protestations of ignorance of politics and with declarations of simplicity of character and outlook, with a claim to inexperience in worldly affairs. Throughout the evening she only once engaged in political conversation, and then she showed a liberal outlook, well maintained in discussion, and based on a conception which was sound.

I was greatly interested by the way the other women greeted her. There were about six women who were present at the dinner or who came in afterwards. All but one of them greeted Mrs. Simpson with a kiss. She received it with appropriate dignity, but in no case did she return it.

The King spoke very plainly about some of his Ministers, making blunt criticisms of this man or that. I, too, spoke freely. There was no mention of the divorce; though, for a moment, I thought there would be when the King took me into another room and closed the door behind him. But he did not refer to the subject and the talk that followed was entirely devoted to personalities.[1] However, on leaving, the King said he wanted to see me later for there was something he wanted to talk about. This showed me that the dinner was leading up to something. We parted just before midnight.

Now the King had asked me on 16th October to do what I could to modify the attitude of the American newspapers, particularly the United Press.[2] I promised to consider that problem. First I had an interview with one of the representatives of the United Press. He asked for assurance that the King did not intend to marry. I decided to place responsibility for an answer—if any—with Mr. Monckton, and I arranged an appointment with him. Mr. Monckton did not keep the appointment and sent a message next day to say that he had been detained by a royal command.

[1] Mainly to a discussion of Baldwin.
[2] An important and reliable American News Agency covering all the capitals of the world.

35

Undoubtedly, a royal command supersedes other appointments,[1] but as I was to see Mr. Monckton about the King's own business, I concluded that the attitude of the American newspapers could not be so very important to the Court after all. In fact, this was not so, but that was how I thought at the time, so I decided to do nothing more about the United Press. I was glad to be out of the affair, for negotiations with the Americans promised to be both difficult and tedious, and quite likely to end in failure.

I believed that my task was at an end and I left for Canada and Arizona by ship via New York on 14th November. However, before going I asked Lord Brownlow to consider telling the King that if he contemplated marriage to Mrs. Simpson, he should disclose his intention to those whom he wished to consult. He was leaving the position too vague in the minds of those about him, and that vagueness might well lead to hurried decisions which would be bad decisions.

On 16th November, when I was two days out at sea, the King sent me a telegram saying he had no idea I was going abroad, and that there was something he had meant to tell me. He now wanted to make the communication. In effect, he was asking me what was to be done.

There was a note of criticism in his message as though it was my duty to inform him before leaving England. But he had no good ground for complaint, for I had announced my intention in Saturday's *Daily Express*, 14th November. I wrote in that newspaper that I was going to my own home where the sun shines all winter long—'to see once more the forests and rivers of that Province of New Brunswick colonised by our Scottish ancestors'.

As I felt no need for self-reproach, I replied to the King's message saying that there had been no want of duty on my

[1] People who are unable to fulfil a Royal Command sometimes put an advertisement in the Personal Column of *The Times* giving the reason. It is an expensive way of advertising the fact that they have been invited to a Royal function.

part. Mr. Monckton had not come to the appointment with me, and I did not know that anything more was required of me. I added that if I was expected to deal with the American Press, I could do that more effectively in New York than in London.

In reply, I was told that my message had been understood and that I would soon hear more. I did hear more, much more. One message after another came from the King.

Pressure was also put on me from several other directions. The effect of it all was to urge me to come back, as I was required to give advice. It was then that I was told that the King intended to marry Mrs. Simpson, that he had informed the Government and that it was clear the Government would be hostile. Although this was the first direct intimation I had received, I was by no means surprised, for my suspicions had been increasingly aroused. I asked if my advice would be required only on the handling of the Press and was told that I would be consulted on the wider issues. I was also told that if I required any more information, I had only to ask for it. I did not ask.

Members of my own staff were also communicating with me. Mr. Michael Wardell, who was a close friend of the King, and Mr. Whelan, my secretary, both cabled me to say that they had been asked to impress on me the need to come to London. There were innumerable telephone conversations between sea and shore, and I was left with the impression that my attendance on the King was sought with a real belief that I could help him in the crisis that was developing. Finally I gave the King a promise to come straight home, and my stay in New York was limited to the daylight hours.

During this waiting interval in New York, I called on my friend Mr. Joseph Patterson of the *Daily News*. While I was in his office, the King got through to me from London on the telephone. I was greatly disturbed by the freedom of his communications, and I tried, without success, to keep the talk on a non-committal level. I believed that the telephone

37

was a dangerous method of telling important secrets, even in the best of circumstances, and when the call was transmitted through a newspaper office it was received in the worst circumstances. The conversation was of course monitored. I asked that secrecy should be observed. Fortunately, Mr. Patterson was a man who would not make public use of a private conversation, but the King was not to know that.

I sailed in the evening by the *Bremen*.[1]

[1] Transatlantic flights were not organized until 1939.

IV

IT WAS only on the way back to England that the full
seriousness and also the possibilities of the situation became
clear to me. When I sailed from England on 14th November,
I believed there was more in the King's mind than he was yet
willing to declare. I was excited, but not surprised, when I
heard of his intention to marry. And I was confused by the
recollection of the previous assurance from an authoritative
source[1] that there was no question of marriage.

The King's disclosure settled all doubt.

As I journeyed across the Atlantic for the second time, I
had full opportunity for reflection. I studied the American
newspapers which I had brought with me for all they had
to say about the affair, and that was a great deal. I had the
benefit of frequent discussions in the ship with a friend who
was wise and experienced in worldly and human affairs,
though not, as it happened, in politics. And I made frequent
use of the sea-to-shore telephone and also of the telegraph.

It appeared to me as a threefold struggle. Political;
Ecclesiastical; Personal.

The political conflict interested me above all other issues.

Constitutionally, the King was free to marry anyone he
liked except a Roman Catholic. The Royal Marriages Act
gave him the power to prohibit the marriage of any member of
the family, no matter what the age of that member might be.[2]

---

[1] See p. 33.

[2] [This is not quite correct. A member of the Royal Family over the
age of 25 who wishes to marry may do so without the Monarch's consent
by giving notice to the Privy Council. The marriage may then take place

But nobody could prohibit the marriage of the King himself.[1]

The Prime Minister, however, had set his face inflexibly against the King's will to marry. He had, without doubt, considered his strength, and weighed his advantages. The battle would be waged to the destruction of the King, or the Prime Minister.

Baldwin's shrewd and cunning judgement of politics would serve him well in these conditions. His caution and his conviction would make him a relentless foe. There were, moreover, positive factors that he could command.

First of all there was his Cabinet, which Baldwin could commit to his cause. He was official Leader of the House of Commons, and he could rely upon the exceedingly faithful and influential pro-Baldwin Press. And in particular he would be sustained and upheld by the authority of the Church which was sure to be frantically and inflexibly hostile to the marriage.

On the King's side, there were compensating and formidable elements. He would be assisted by a few experienced and informed friends who could rely on a great mass of public support. There was the possibility too that the unity of parties would be challenged, with the chance that a new Prime Minister appealing for support would find adherents from both sides of the House, shattering Party structures.

Then again, the King's counsellors would draw strength and comfort from the marked weakness of Baldwin. For the Prime Minister was discredited in his public career. He had recently informed the House that he had deceived and misled the electors in order to win the election of 1935. This confession was made in reply to a devastating speech in the Com-

after twelve months, unless within that period both Houses of Parliament have expressly declared their disapproval of the marriage.—Ed.]

[1] This was true at the time, but it may not be true any longer. The Abdication has set a precedent and henceforth no British King will contemplate marriage without the consent of his Government. The Royal Prerogative has suffered a further and drastic reduction.

mons by Lloyd George. Baldwin said he would use 'appalling frankness' and admitted that he had concealed the need for a great armaments drive because to tell the truth would have lost him the election. Though he tried afterwards to wriggle out of an admission which shocked every member of the Commons, his own election speeches were brought against him. They left him without a shred of excuse or any defence at all.[1]

Baldwin had also confessed to misinforming the Members about the air strength of Germany. He had become an object of ridicule. Low's cartoon of 'Sealed Lips' had been taken up in the music-halls, and Baldwin was the butt of the comedians.[2]

It appeared to me his end was in sight. He was politically distrusted. He would shortly go down in disgrace.

I had my own reasons for hoping that this would be the case. Baldwin had never held any faith in an Economic Empire,[3] and on the great design of a united Empire prospering within its own tariff barrier, I had struggled against him for thirteen long years. This cause had brought me to

[1] [This is not correct. Baldwin said that he had not advocated great armaments in 1933, for fear of public opinion. By waiting until 1935, he had then been able to win the general election on a rearmament ticket.—Ed.]

[2] Baldwin's exact words were: 'My lips are not yet unsealed.' But this was promptly turned by the public into the neater form, 'My lips are sealed.' The Low cartoons showing Baldwin with sticking-plaster over his mouth were immensely popular, and very damaging to Baldwin.

[3] Baldwin opposed the Empire policy because it meant taxes on foreign food. He often said that it was not he who opposed foreign food taxes, but the electorate which would never tolerate them. He compared food taxes to an attractive Newfoundland dog. If you give the slightest encouragement to the dog, it plants its paws on your white waistcoat which is ruined for ever. Baldwin was determined to preserve his political white waistcoat, which was his majority. But without taxes on foreign food and free imports of Empire food, Imperial Economic Union was an impossibility, for there were large parts of the Empire, entirely agricultural, which produced nothing but food. Without taxes on foreign food there could be no advantage for food-producing Dominions and Colonies.

41

England in 1910, to begin a life-struggle for economic union between Britain and the rest of the Empire, comparable to the union of the American states. This cause had brought me into politics.

Yet in taking this view of Baldwin's political chances in an open contest with the King, I did not enter the struggle to dislodge the Prime Minister from Downing Street. That would be a welcome by-product of my efforts. But I was striving to help the King because I believed he had the right to command support and because his cause was just. My efforts would be primarily directed to helping safeguard the Throne and trying to secure for the King freedom to marry the woman of his choice, a freedom enjoyed by the humblest of his subjects. An attempt to deny that freedom to any subject would have been called intolerance. I called it intolerance when the attempt was made against the King.

My meditation led me to believe that on the political issue the King must prevail and Baldwin must be destroyed. Short of persuading the Commons to pass a Bill of Deposition, which was impossible, there was little that the Prime Minister could do, if the King played his cards well.

The ecclesiastical front, on the other hand, would be a serious and probably indestructible obstacle to the King's wish to marry the woman of his choice.

As I understood it, the opposition of the Church of England would be based on the sacramental character of marriage. The Church regarded marriage as indissoluble, except by death.

Edward VIII was a member of the Church of England. By the Act of Settlement of 1701, the Sovereign is bound to be a member of that Church. The King is officially designated as 'Defender of the Faith'. There is a widespread but erroneous belief that the Monarch is the 'Head' of the Church of England. This is not so.[1] But there was no doubt that the King

[1] Henry VIII did assume the title of 'Head' of the Church of England, but it was abrogated by Mary Tudor, who was, of course, a Catholic, and

must expect the most tenacious opposition and the most active hostility if he ventured on a marriage to a woman with two living husbands.

His Majesty, as 'Defender of the Faith', might be subject to excommunication. Possibly refusal to administer communion, as in the incidents following the marriage of the 9th Duke of Marlborough, could and would result in a sustained and vociferous demand for abdication. How could divines call down God's blessing upon a man who, in their conception, was living in sin? Again, what of the prayers for other members of the Royal Family which, according to ancient custom, is the Order of Church Service? Would God be asked to bless the junior members of the Royal House while consigning the Head of the family to exclusion?

These were nice considerations—the most serious being the Church of England's powers of excommunication. What would be the position if the King married Mrs. Simpson, and the Archbishop exercised his authority of excommunication?[1] A most curious situation would develop. Some would maintain that Edward VIII would have lost his right to be King. Others would never tolerate the Church challenging the King's title to reign.

Different attitudes too prevailed among the non-conformist members of the King's subjects.[2] The Westminster Confession of Faith which governs the Church of Scotland as by Law Established, defines the marriage relationship as a contract and not a sacrament. In the Presbyterian interpretation of

when Elizabeth I succeeded to the Throne, she was contented with a much more modest role than her father had claimed. Briefly, she held authority as the temporal (not spiritual) guardian and protector of the Church.

[1] There was, as it happened, little cause for apprehension. If the King persisted in his marriage plans, the Archbishop of Canterbury had evidently decided to perform the Coronation Service. His refusal, wrote Lockhart, his biographer, would otherwise have consigned the leadership of the Church to another prelate of 'fumbling and suspected' hands (Lockhart: *Cosmo Gordon Lang*, p. 399).

[2] In Britain, there were more church-goers in the non-conformist faith than in the Established Church.

43

marriage, the innocent party in a divorce suit incurs no word of blame. Nor is there anything in the law of the Church of Scotland forbidding a Minister to remarry the guilty person. It is customary for a minister to satisfy himself that the sinner sincerely repents. If the minister is assured that the repentance is genuine, he may perform the marriage ceremony. Some Scottish Divines rejected this view and followed the English customs, but they were guilty of heresy.

In the Dominions, of course, there was no Establishment, and Presbyterianism, in one form or another, was at least as powerful as Anglicanism. In the Dominions, the contractual view of marriage was accepted in ordinary social life, whatever any Church might say.

The ecclesiastical viewpoint was bound to produce interesting divisions in Parliament. Anglican Members would give considerable weight to the opinion that the King, by virtue of his office as a member of that Church, must do nothing incompatible with Anglican dogma. But the Scottish contingent was entitled to point out that the King, when he was in Scotland, was a member of the Church of Scotland, which did recognize divorce.

In any calculation, the Church must prove the real focus of opposition and hostility to the King's plans. No matter. I did not accept this narrow restriction in marriage. The opposition of the clergy would not prejudice me in my conduct and attitude to the crisis.

Finally, persons must be considered, as in every human drama. Mrs. Simpson was not a popular name in West End circles. Her little band of friends was small and not influential.

The aristocratic families of Britain had not taken up with her. She would be a burden and a heavy load to carry. But the King would spread his covering wings about her, and that protection must brush away many troubles.

Queen Mary might be more important than Priest or Politician. She was much respected and greatly admired. If she entered into the arena maybe her presence would do heavy damage to the marriage project.

Lastly the House of York was popular. The Duke would make a success of monarchy. He was held in the highest esteem. His influence would please both State and Church.

This balance-sheet of doubts and benefits gave sound reasons for optimism. But after everything had been entered up on either side of the ledger, the most exciting possibility depended on the conduct of two men—the King and Baldwin. In the preliminary movements now developing into open political warfare absolutely everything depended upon His Majesty's resolution, determination and steadfastness of purpose. Insistence on marriage would leave the hostile politicians in a state of impotence. Their only hope would be in the mobilization of public opinion against the Throne.

Any movement in that direction would be blocked and beaten down by the combined efforts of the forces of Rothermere and me. We controlled sufficient net sales of newspapers to blast and frustrate the knavish tricks of the enemies of the Crown. And I felt sure and certain that Lord Rothermere would join me in a full-blooded campaign. Baldwin would no doubt make use of the radio. But the King would have the right to the same opportunities as his enemy.

Then there was that mighty weapon which counted large in the political estimation against Baldwin, Attlee and the whole hierarchy of politics. If the Prime Minister resigned, a new Government formed in sympathy with the King's desire to marry the woman of his heart would draw strength from the back benches of both Tories, Socialists, and even the tiny little band of Liberals.

Thus the prospects of the collapse of two great political parties would follow and a new group taking over the affairs of state might become a successor to both Tories and Socialists, consigning the big shots of these organizations to tiny splinter followings. Baldwin, with his ministers all about him greedy for power, would hesitate for long before facing such an upheaval.

This weapon could be used with such advantage that I convinced myself, on that long sea journey in a German bottom, that the King had only to persevere in order to prevail.

V

ON ARRIVING back in England I drove immediately to Fort
Belvedere where the King met me at the door. He brought
me to a room where he had had a special lunch prepared,
according to the diet which I then followed.

Much had happened in my absence. On 20th October, four
days after I had first had an audience with the King, Baldwin
had come to see him.[1] In seeking an audience Baldwin did
no more than his duty, but when he came to the one vital
issue, he shied at the fence and did much less. Instead of
asking about the marriage, he asked for a whisky and soda.
Fortified by the drink, he worked his way round to suggesting
that the King should endeavour to stop the divorce hearing
at Ipswich.

The King replied that he could not ask Mrs. Simpson to
sacrifice her legal rights because of her friendship with himself. That was a perfectly proper reply provided the King had
no feelings towards her except those of friendship. If he had
deeper feelings, and an intention to marry, it was no reply
at all. But the King kept his own counsel, and the Prime
Minister, having edged around the subject, stayed to talk
about the roses.[2]

There was a certain failure of candour on the King's part.
Certainly there was deceit and dishonesty on the part of the
Prime Minister. For he knew at the time the intention of the

---

[1] Baldwin had spent the previous weekend with Lord Fitzalan. The
King's Secretary, Hardinge, was present.
[2] The Duke's version of the interview is given in *A King's Story*, pp.
316–18.

King to marry Mrs. Simpson and he concealed that knowledge from his Sovereign.[1] The question that should have been asked was not asked. The answer that should have been volunteered was not given.

Both King and Prime Minister came out of this interview with discredit. They did not approach the problem about to shake the nation and the Empire with any measure of sincerity.

The Audience had proved most unsatisfactory and Baldwin did not press for another meeting.

He now set out on a canvass for support.

He had already received encouragement from Lord Kemsley, the powerful newspaper proprietor. He called a meeting of MacDonald, Chamberlain, Halifax, Simon and Runciman for the purpose of ascertaining the attitude of the Free Churches.[2] Here it may be said that Halifax was a curious source of Free Church dispositions. He was in fact a fanatical High Churchman and of course violently critical of divorce and remarriage. He must have been present to 'make weight' for Baldwin.

Baldwin saw Mr. Gwynne of the *Morning Post* and Sir Frederick Maurice of the British Legion. He talked with Attlee, leader of the Opposition, receiving assurances of support. Sir Archibald Sinclair, Liberal leader, was consulted with a similar result.

Baldwin also saw Vincent Massey, High Commissioner for Canada. He found Massey's views were 'sound enough' but, reflecting the opinions of the Prime Minister of Canada, in doubt and hesitation about the proper course for the Dominions.[3] Mr. Bruce of Australia was ill in bed. He was however interviewed by Dawson.[4]

It was not until 16th November, two days after I sailed for

[1] See Viscount Templewood (Sir Samuel Hoare), *Nine Troubled Years*, p. 215.
[2] Young: *Stanley Baldwin*, pp. 235–7.
[3] Wrench: *Geoffrey Dawson and Our Times*, p. 346.
[4] *History of the Times*, Vol. 4, Part II, p. 1033.

Canada in the *Bremen*, that the King told the Prime Minister what he meant to do.

Now, in Fort Belvedere, he told his story fully and frankly to me, and he told it very well.

He began by saying that he intended to marry Mrs. Simpson. If the Government would make no concession to the marriage there would be no Coronation. 'No marriage, no Coronation.' He said these words emphatically, rapping on the table to drive home his point, as if to show that this particular decision was settled and beyond discussion.

He mentioned a letter he had received on 13th November from his Secretary, Major the Hon. Alexander Hardinge, which recited:

(1) That the silence of the British Press on the subject of Mrs. Simpson would be broken and that there would be an outburst in a few days.

(2) That the Prime Minister and Senior Members of the Government were meeting to decide on action. Resignation of the Government could not be excluded.

(3) That an alternative Government, he had 'reason to know', was impossible.

(4) That the only other course was a dissolution and a General Election when the chief issue would be Mrs. Simpson.

(5) That Mrs. Simpson must go abroad without delay.

(6) That the matter was of great urgency due to the attitude of the Press.

The King summed up by saying 'Who could have told Alex Hardinge all this but the Prime Minister?'[1]

The King told me of his second interview with Baldwin on 16th November when he had informed Baldwin of his marriage intentions. He explained that Baldwin had 'advised'

[1] Hardinge has since written that his letter to the King was a result of what Baldwin had told him the night before. (*Before the Abdication*, by Lord Hardinge (*The Times*, 29th November, 1955).)

against the marriage and had told the King that if he meant to go on with it, he had better abdicate for neither the nation nor the Empire would accept Mrs. Simpson as Queen. The King went on to say that he had asked Mr. Baldwin to consult with his Cabinet colleagues, having a belief that some of the younger members would stand by him. He also said to Mr. Baldwin that he would like to talk personally with Sir Samuel Hoare and Mr. Duff Cooper. Baldwin had agreed to this and the interviews had taken place forthwith.

He told me that Sir Samuel Hoare had given him no encouragement at all, but he still had hopes of Mr. Duff Cooper. Mr. Duff Cooper had urged delay of marriage for a year or perhaps for longer, but the King believed he could be relied upon to speak for him in the Cabinet.

He then said that on 21st November Mr. Esmond Harmsworth had taken Mrs. Simpson to lunch and had propounded to her the project of a morganatic marriage.[1] Mrs. Simpson, the King said, preferred the morganatic marriage to any other solution of the problem. He told me also that Mr. Harmsworth had laid the morganatic proposal before Mr. Baldwin and he understood that it originally came from Mr. Churchill.[2]

In speaking of Mr. Harmsworth, the King confessed to

[1] [The *Concise Oxford Dictionary* defines a morganatic marriage as 'one between man of exalted rank and woman of lower rank, who remains in her former station, the issue having no claim to succeed to possessions or title of father'. Though the practice is common on the Continent, there has been no case of a morganatic marriage in this country. The members of the Royal Family, such as the Duke of Cambridge and the Duke of Sussex, who are sometimes described as having been morganatically married, had not fulfilled the requirements of the Royal Marriage Act and were legally not married at all. Baldwin was therefore correct when he said in Parliament: 'There is no such thing as what is called a Morganatic Marriage known to our law.' He omitted to add that things hitherto unknown can be made law by Act of Parliament.—Ed.]

[2] [The idea of the morganatic marriage actually originated with Collin Brooks, an adviser of Lord Rothermere's. He mentioned it as a possible (rather than obvious or easy) solution. Rothermere seized upon the idea and passed it to his son, Esmond.—Ed.]

some embarrassment. Harmsworth had asked him if I was returning home, and the King had not told him that he himself had recalled me. He asked me to protect him on this point.

Next, in order to impress me still more with the possibilities of the morganatic scheme, he told me that Lord Rothermere,[1] proprietor of the *Daily Mail*, had promised to give the project his unflinching support.

He told me further that Mr. Baldwin had consulted Mr. Attlee, who was then the Leader of the Opposition, and had reported him as being unfavourable to the morganatic marriage. However, the King thought that Mr. Attlee's attitude had been misinterpreted, and he did not believe that the Labour members of the House of Commons would be hostile in the long run.[2] He went on generally to argue that the morganatic marriage was a reasonable proposal and that it should be acceded to, and he expressed the belief that there would be a great deal of support for it among the younger members of the Cabinet.

I then gave my recommendations. They were as follows.

Withdraw the plan for a morganatic marriage at once. It would be rejected by the Government. I was emphatic on this point.

Why did I make this recommendation and make it so strongly? Because the request for permission to make a morganatic marriage would place the King in the hands of Baldwin and the other politicians. The politicians had no status at all in the main issue of marriage. The King was free to marry whom he chose[3] and the Government had no power in law or in precedent to forbid the banns.

[1] Lord Rothermere was more than a great newspaper proprietor. He was a man of courage. He was endowed with a public spirit, and he displayed unbounded generosity.

[2] Attlee was not well disposed to His Majesty. He tells in his autobiography that he informed Baldwin his party would not approve of Mrs. Simpson, with the exception of a few of the intelligentsia 'who can be trusted to take the wrong view on any subject' (*As It Happened*, p. 86).

[3] [Short of marrying a Roman Catholic.—Ed.]

51

But he was not free to make a morganatic marriage, because such a marriage was unknown in English law, and could only be made possible by act of Parliament. By proposing such a marriage, the King was asking for legislation, and it was only the Prime Minister who could grant or refuse Parliamentary time for the necessary Bill. If he refused then the King (1) must accept an open humiliation and the jeopardizing of his marriage, or else he (2) must dismiss his Ministers and seek new advisers in the House of Commons who would give him the support he required.

At the same time, I tried to soften this very unpalatable advice against the morganatic marriage by saying that the King should not necessarily refuse such an offer if it eventually came from the Government. The King was in an exceedingly strong position. His intended marriage might be highly distasteful to the Executive, but the Executive had no powers to prevent it. If the Executive thought that a morganatic marriage would make things easier for themselves and would avert their own resignation, then they might propose it and the King might consider it. If he accepted, he could not be asking for a favour, but rather granting one. He would not be playing into Baldwin's hands. Let it come from the Government or the Press, but not from the King.

Coupled with this advice were two other recommendations. I advised the King to find some friend in the Cabinet who would represent his case, and advised him also not to let the Cabinet reach any decision on any issue until he had measured the strength on either side. I then said that I would discuss these suggestions with Mr. Monckton if the King approved of them.

The King then said that he approved of my recommendations and so I took my leave to go back to London and consult with others about putting the recommendations into effect. I joined Mr. Michael Wardell, who was waiting for me. On the way back to London I talked things over with him. On arriving in town I had an interview with Mr.

52

Monckton.[1] He fell in with my views in a way that struck me as more convincing than the agreement the King had already expressed. Although the King had appeared to accept all I recommended, I was not entirely sure of him. I had the impression he would certainly consult Mrs. Simpson and that his agreement was contingent on her opinion also being in favour of my views. But Mr. Monckton appeared to me to be heartily in favour of abandoning the proposal for a morganatic marriage. I was strengthened by his common sense and sound judgement on the whole issue of the marriage plan.

Although it was growing late in the evening when I concluded my meeting with Mr. Monckton, I drove straight to the Admiralty where I saw Sir Samuel Hoare,[2] hoping to persuade him to be the advocate for the King within the Cabinet. I pointed out to him that this would not involve any approval of the course the King proposed to take. He would simply be an advocate representing the King's point of view. If the King were given fair representation and a fair hearing, I thought the marriage could be postponed until after an interval of mature consideration and informed discussions. My object was to get rid of the morganatic marriage proposal and to gain time for the King, so that he could weigh the effects of his marriage intentions on men of importance who could interpret public opinion. Sir Samuel Hoare replied that he did not want to play the role that I proposed for him. He was against a morganatic marriage, or any other marriage, and if the King persisted with his intention he would be in favour of abdication. However, he promised to talk with his friends in the Cabinet and see me again next day.

[1] Throughout the Crisis, Mr. Monckton played a most active part, going very far beyond the normal duties of a legal adviser. In fact, he took the place of the King's own Private Secretary, Major the Hon. Alexander Hardinge—who had declared against the King before the battle commenced.

[2] Sir Samuel Hoare was First Lord of the Admiralty.

I had considered the possibility that nobody in the Cabinet would be willing to act as the King's spokesman, and with that in mind I had suggested to the King that if he found it impossible to get an advocate in the Cabinet some prominent citizen outside of politics should be asked to put the King's case to Mr. Baldwin. The man I proposed was Lord Hewart, then Lord Chief Justice, and the King approved of the idea.[1]

This suggestion came to nothing because of the rapid changes in the situation. I believed throughout that time, sympathetic treatment, patience and endurance would bring the King safely through the crisis of his love story. My hope was that the morganatic project might be abandoned and that the King might be advised by wise counsellors and prominent men who were sympathetic to him, but determined on avoiding abdication.

But my first hopes were at once to be dashed. I had got home to Stornoway House and was asleep in bed at two in the morning when the King telephoned. A conversation took place that greatly embarrassed me. The King spoke, as on a previous occasion, with such freedom that I was positively alarmed, and he, in turn, was impatient of the guarded nature of my replies.

He was anxious to hear the outcome of my talk with Hoare. I made an evasive reply, for it was too early to say anything definite, as I had to see Hoare again next day. In any event, I was not prepared to go over the ground on the telephone. The King was hardly satisfied with my reply.

I urged him most earnestly not to make the telephone the

[1] Hewart was an old friend of mine. We were in Parliament together and I heard him make his maiden speech, before the first War. It was a very able effort. He became Attorney-General in Lloyd George's Coalition Government. He was a most successful Parliamentarian. When the office of Lord Chief Justice became vacant, Hewart asked for it. He was entitled to the succession. But Lloyd George resisted, promising that after another year or two Hewart would get the job. Meanwhile there was a stop-gap appointment. After several months, Hewart claimed the office for the second time, and Bonar Law insisted. Thus Hewart became Lord Chief Justice.

means of such very private communications. He asked me if I suspected that we might be overheard, and said that if his telephone was tapped, that was the end of everything. I said there were other dangers to privacy. We might be overheard merely through crossed wires, but, in any event, I believed that there were unauthorized listeners here and there.[1]

The King then told me again he approved of my plan and endorsed my recommendations. But, he added, Mrs. Simpson preferred the morganatic marriage to any other solution. Indeed if the choice were between becoming Queen and being a morganatic wife she would choose the latter. When he made this statement I knew that the agreement between us was null and void. Whatever he might assent to in his mind, it would not have the agreement of his heart. I no longer expected him to withdraw the proposition of a morganatic marriage from the Cabinet. And he did not withdraw it.

It was now obvious that the prospects were clouded with doubt and uncertainty. The fatal weaknesses of the King's position were rapidly becoming apparent. His anxiety was intense but he was anxious about the wrong things—all his energies should have been devoted to the main issue, which was the struggle to remain on the Throne and to marry in due time. If he had carried out a well organized campaign, he would have attained his end and finished Baldwin politically for ever. But he was preoccupied with other things, principally with protecting Mrs. Simpson from hostile publicity, or indeed from publicity of any kind, at whatever cost or sacrifice.

His position was isolated. During his brilliantly successful

[1] Were telephones tapped? Lord Brownlow stated that a telegram to Nice was intercepted and sold to the newspapers. He said that conversations between London and Cannes were intercepted at the British end. He complained to Sir John Simon, Secretary of State for Home Affairs, who was ignorant of any such interference. Mr. Goddard, Mrs. Simpson's solicitor, declared that others were aware of the Cannes–London telephone conversations between Mrs. Simpson and the King.

career as Prince of Wales he had made friends almost everywhere except in the political world where he now most sorely needed them. He had mixed more freely with the people than any Heir Apparent had ever done before, but he had hardly mixed at all with politicians. As a result he had friends in coal-mines, but not in the Cabinet. His interests were never political. They were social in both senses of the term. They were social in the sense that he liked sports, parties and the company of brisk and lively people. They were also social in the sense that he was deeply interested in conditions of ordinary life and work, and in the expansion of British export trade in the markets of the world.

But he was now facing a grave political problem quite unprepared for the task, and he was neglecting to follow the advice of his own counsellors and was also neglecting to consult sage and experienced friends to whom he might have turned. Even his legal advisers were at that time quite inexperienced in politics. He should have clung to the main purpose of staying on the Throne. If that had happened all else would have followed — but that demanded patience, not impatience. It demanded delay, not hasty and impulsive actions.

'Ask me for anything except time,' said Napoleon. The thing that the fighting soldier could not grant, the King of Britain should have been able to command — but the King could not command it. Time was denied him and everything fell to ruin.

VI

WHEN THE King telephoned me late at night and told me Mrs. Simpson preferred morganatic marriage to becoming Queen, I knew my urgings were in vain. A morganatic marriage was what Mrs. Simpson wanted, and what Mrs. Simpson wanted was what the King wanted. However, I continued to press His Majesty to abandon his request to the Government for legislation implementing a morganatic marriage.

Although henceforth he consistently and positively rejected this advice, I still served in the struggle to avoid the tragedy of Abdication. Baldwin would certainly press the King to abandon marriage or give up his Throne. Refusal and rejection of the Prime Minister's advice would automatically result in resignation of the Government.

If Baldwin did resign, what next? Had the King any hopes of finding a political leader willing and able to form an alternative government that would be more friendly disposed towards himself?

There was no hope from any members of the Baldwin Cabinet. They had all been pledged to stand by their chief. If he went, they would all go and no doubt would be committed not to serve under anybody else. There was equally no hope from the official Opposition, for Mr. Attlee had given Baldwin an undertaking of support.

But there was also the Liberal Party. Its Parliamentary leader was Sir Archibald Sinclair. His following in Parliament was small, but he had many friends and, what was more important, he had no enemies. He was universally respected

57

for his high gifts of mind and character. If he had agreed to form and to lead an all-Party Administration, he would have commanded wide support and provoked no hostility. It goes without saying that such an Administration would have done much to restore the waning fortunes of the Liberal Party.

But it was not to be. Sir Archibald Sinclair had a strong bias towards the Non-Conformist Conscience and he, like Mr. Attlee, had joined the 'no marriage' front. I was told at the time that he had done so, and I wrote to him later to ask if it was true. Sir Archibald replied, on 24th August, 1951:

'It is true that Mr. Baldwin consulted me about the King's proposal to marry Mrs. Simpson and again on two or three other occasions about the development of the crisis, and the proposed morganatic marriage. I thought that the morganatic marriage was an unsatisfactory compromise. It would offend Puritan opinion which still survives in this country (especially in the Liberal Party) and the controversy would not be settled but would be revived whenever questions arose about the rights and status of the morganatic wife—the King always pressing to enlarge and his critics to restrict them. I also urged the importance of consultation with the Dominions, for I feared that a morganatic marriage (especially with a lady who had been in the divorce courts) would weaken the position of the monarchy not only at home but also as a link between the nations of the Empire.'

Thus, acting from these motives, this distinguished and popular man had rejected the glittering opportunity that was offered to his Party.

The situation was difficult but by no means impossible. The Socialist and Liberal leaders were out of the question, but there was still a promising chance that an eminent backbencher might form an Administration which would draw support from members of all Parties and particularly from the back-bench Tories. Destiny appeared to point to Winston Churchill.

Churchill would and could form a Government. His appearance as Prime Minister would have put an end to talk of Abdication. Marriage would have been another matter. Churchill would not have been in any position to oppose the union. But he might have found ways of reconciling the King to a long delay with all the chances of another and different outcome.

Of course he had disadvantages. His personal following in Parliament was small and he was unpopular with a proportion of the Tory Members because of his uncompromising stand on rearmament.[1] But he was the greatest figure on the Parliamentary scene and there was no doubt that he could form a Government well able to hold its own. He could have secured the co-operation of Lloyd George, the only man in Parliament whose talents and personal authority rivalled his own. The Ministers who resigned along with Baldwin might well find themselves left high and dry, and it would not be long till they drifted back to the fold.[2] Churchill was not the ideal man from my point of view for he had never subscribed to the Empire faith, but he was undoubtedly the best man to step into the gap that Baldwin's resignation would have created. Accordingly I set to work, seeking to rally support for His Majesty.

But the situation was gravely worsened on 25th November. It was on that day that the morganatic plan took on a most disastrous aspect. Malcolm MacDonald, Secretary of State for the Dominions, had reminded Baldwin that legislation in

[1] Indeed, in succeeding years, the hostility of the Party machine to Churchill grew so great that there was even a move to unseat him in his own constituency. He won with a majority of two to one in his constituency committee, but that left a very strong minority against him.

[2] That is what happened in 1922 after the Carlton Club meeting when the majority of Tory M.P.s left the leaders, Austen Chamberlain and Birkenhead. These men were faithful to Lloyd George and were not included in the new and purely Tory Administration under Bonar Law. But they rejoined the Conservative Cabinet before long.

providing for a morganatic marriage would require corresponding measures in some of the Dominions. Baldwin saw at once that if his question were framed in blunt and uncompromising terms those Dominions would say No. Baldwin therefore informed the King that his request would have to be referred to all the Dominions as well as to the British Cabinet. He asked if the King wished him to make this reference. The King answered 'Yes'—and thereby sealed his own fate.

The message to the Dominions was sent out on 27th November. It was cunningly framed. Professor Mansergh[1] tells us that Baldwin gave to the Dominions 'an account of his interviews with the King and the alternatives of ordinary marriage, morganatic marriage, and abdication in favour of the Duke of York that had now to be considered. He recorded in the telegram the views he had already expressed to the King, and asked the dominion Prime Ministers for their personal opinions on the course that should be followed and also for their assessments of the likely views of their peoples. Whether in this he was constitutionally correct is open to doubt.'

Baldwin had given his own version of the crisis. He put forward his own arguments. The King's case was not stated. Thus it was that a prejudiced and misleading account of the King's request to his own Prime Minister was sent out to the Dominions in the form that is commonly called 'loaded dice'.

Sir Samuel Hoare visited me on Thursday, 26th November. But he made no mention of the intention to refer the morganatic marriage issue to the Dominions. The King telephoned me that night. He said not a word about the conversation with Baldwin concerning the fatal message.

There was a Cabinet Meeting on Friday, 27th November, which approved the words of Baldwin's message to the Dominions, that were really words of disaster for the King.

[1] Mansergh: *Survey of British Commonwealth Affairs*, Vol. II (ii), p. 43.

Sir Samuel Hoare came to visit me after the Ministers' meeting was over.

Hoare did not surprise me at all when he confirmed his refusal to speak for the King in the Cabinet. He said he would take no active steps against the King, but he thought it better he should have a firm refusal at once.

This was only what I expected but the news of the reference to the Dominions, which Hoare gave to me, was a great surprise and shock. I made all haste to the Palace, thinking there was still time to alter this fatal decision, for I believed that the message was not yet sent out. However, Baldwin got his message to the Dominions nearly as quickly as I could get to the Palace.

My interview with the King was profoundly unsatisfactory. He confirmed the bad news. He also showed that he understood very clearly how Baldwin would frame the question—'Do you recommend the King's marriage to a woman with two husbands living, or do you recommend Abdication?' Anyone who knew the Dominions must recognize at once that 'Abdication' would be the answer to the final question.

I emphasized to the King that there could be no hope of securing popular support for the morganatic marriage unless opinion was carefully prepared by judicious propaganda. I also pointed out that he had the right, under the Statute of Westminster,[1] of sending out his own question, framed in his own terms, in the manner most favourable to himself. He was under no compulsion to let Baldwin put the question for him and put it in such a way that the replies were bound to be unfavourable to the King. But unless the reference to the Dominions was stopped at once seventy-five Ministers (more or less) would know of the King's intentions and no secret could possibly be kept amongst so many. It would become

[1] The Statute of Westminster defines the relationship of the Monarch with the Dominions. Its effect is to place Dominions Prime Ministers on a substantial equality with the British Prime Minister in their relations with the Monarch.

61

publicly known that the King had been refused permission by the British Cabinet to marry the woman of his choice and it would be morally impossible for him to remain on the Throne, a discredited man who had abandoned his intended wife.

The King saw all this—but he did nothing. The reference to the Dominions was not withdrawn. The King did not exercise his right to put the question in his own terms. He did not see the question that Baldwin sent. He did not even see the answers. He followed a policy of total drift which carried him inevitably to disaster.

When the King asked Baldwin about the Dominion replies, Baldwin answered that they were not all in yet, but that they were generally unfavourable. Australia, where Mr. Lyons was Prime Minister,[1] had sent a particularly hostile answer, and Baldwin made haste to show that reply, and no other, to the King.[2]

But he made no mention of the New Zealand reply. Mr. Savage, the Prime Minister, although also a Roman Catholic, had failed to express any real opposition to the morganatic marriage.[3] Baldwin therefore took immediate measures to secure a reply favourable to his own designs. A New Zealand Minister in London was interviewed and asked for an answer hostile to the King.[4]

It was also known that Mr. Mackenzie King, the Prime Minister of Canada, had been canvassed. He was on a visit to London in late October. On 23rd October he spent the night at Chequers with Baldwin,[5] and was informed of the pending divorce of Mrs. Simpson and discussed its implications. On the morning of 27th October, Mr. King attended a Council at the Palace at which Lord Brownlow was also

[1] Mr. Lyons was a Roman Catholic.
[2] Lockhart: *Cosmo Gordon Lang*, p. 402.
[3] See Mansergh: *Survey of British Commonwealth Affairs*, Vol. II (ii), p. 44.
[4] Private information.
[5] Young: *Stanley Baldwin*, p. 235.

THE HON. ALEXANDER HARDINGE:
HE FIRED THE FIRST SHOT

CHAMPIONS OF MORALITY:
GEOFFREY DAWSON AND LADY ASTOR

DR. BLUNT: HE ADMONISHED THE KING

STANLEY BALDWIN: KING MAKER AND BREAKER
(AND IN THE BACKGROUND WALTER MONCKTON)

MONCKTON AGAIN, OR IS IT MR. A?

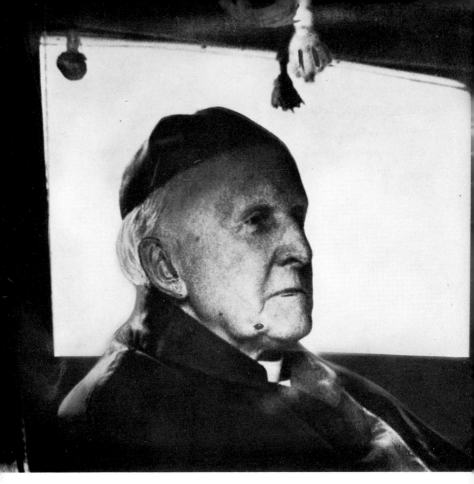

FACE OF A VICTOR: COSMO GORDON LANG,
ARCHBISHOP OF CANTERBURY, ARRIVING
FOR THE ACCESSION COUNCIL

DISREGARDED SPOKESMAN OF PUBLIC OPINION

ANOTHER NEGLECTED PROTEST

present. Shortly after 2 p.m. on that same day, Mrs. Simpson was granted her decree *nisi* at Ipswich. After the Council, Mackenzie King had an audience with His Majesty. He told the King of the love and affection in which he was held by the Canadian people. The Monarch gained the impression that Mr. King felt that the King's relations with Mrs. Simpson were of a purely personal nature and not a public matter.[1]

However, both Baldwin and Geoffrey Dawson of *The Times* joined in making sure of support from Ottawa.[2]

Baldwin's crowning piece of hypocrisy over the Dominions was indulged shortly before his death in 1947. He then told Lockhart that the decisive factor in the King's downfall 'was the uncompromising stand of the Dominion Premiers, and especially of the Prime Minister of Australia.'[3] To such an assertion, Professor Mansergh gives this answer:

'. . . support for a course of action already clearly chartered is not the same thing as a determination of that course'.[4]

[1] *A King's Story*, p. 319 and Young: *Stanley Baldwin*, p. 235.
[2] Young: *Stanley Baldwin*, p. 235 and *History of the Times*, Vol. 4, part II, p. 1028.
[3] Lockhart, *Cosmo Gordon Lang*, p. 404.
[4] Mansergh: *Survey of British Commonwealth Affairs*, Vol. II (ii), p. 44.

VII

TIME WAS now desperately short. Every day increased the urgency of the situation. I saw Hoare again at Stornoway House on Sunday, 29th November. He dined with me and told me that an outburst of publicity in the Press could not be long delayed. I was well aware of this fact. He also told me that the Cabinet would meet on Wednesday, 2nd December, to reach a final decision on the King's request for morganatic legislation. I knew that if a decision was reached it must be against the King and a head-on clash would be inevitable.

This must be avoided. I therefore saw the King again on Monday, 30th November, and made a fresh proposal. Let him withdraw the whole question of his marriage, not merely the request for morganatic legislation. Let him tell Baldwin that, for the moment, he wanted no advice at all, on his marriage intentions. That was a perfectly reasonable request for the Simpson divorce decree could not become absolute for another five months,[1] and that period could most profitably be used in preparing public opinion. Also, it was possible that Baldwin's discredited Government would fall before long.

The interview was long, and the King declared over and over again that he intended to make the marriage, on the Throne or off it. 'Mrs. Simpson,' he declared, 'will not be abandoned.' But he did consent to my proposal and instruc-

[1] At that time an interval of six months had to elapse between the granting of a decree *nisi* and the rendering of that decree 'absolute'. The divorce did not take effect till the decree absolute was granted.

ted Mr. Monckton to tell Baldwin that the King wanted no advice on the marriage.

On the same day, 30th November, as directed by the King, I saw Churchill at five o'clock and gave him a detailed account of my conversations with the King. The objections to a morganatic marriage were canvassed. Churchill had been specifically and positively banned by Baldwin from audience with the King. The Prime Minister's constitutional position gave him the right to decide who should be permitted to give advice to the Monarch. The interdiction of Churchill, however, did not interrupt my telling the King of Churchill's observations on the crisis. And on several occasions I made full use of my latitude. After I had spoken with Churchill, I saw Sir Samuel Hoare at half-past six.

That night, Mr. Monckton told me he had received instructions from the King to inform Baldwin that he wished to withdraw the request for advice on his marriage.

On Tuesday, 1st December, Mr. Monckton told me of his interview with Baldwin. When he delivered his message Baldwin asked if this represented any change of attitude by the King—in other words did it mean that the marriage was to be abandoned? Mr. Monckton replied that he had no instructions on this point, and Baldwin thereafter ignored the King's request. He went on as if it had never been made.

This Tuesday was the last day of the Press silence. It was on that day that Bishop Blunt of Bradford made the speech that touched off the publicity gunpowder barrel. He deplored the King's alleged inattention to religious matters, and the *Yorkshire Post* and other Northern newspapers not only printed the speech but made editorial comment on it. This comment did not appear to the public till the morning of 2nd December, but I saw it the night before and communicated it to the King.[1] At the same time I asked him to release

---

[1] The Archbishop has been blamed for inspiring Bishop Blunt's speech. He denied that any instigation came from him. But the Archbishop did summon all the Bishops to London just before the Blunt speech and

the restrictions that he had imposed on the Press that was favourable to himself. He refused.

Now that publicity had broken out, Baldwin worked hard to secure a unanimous Press in his favour. He even commissioned Hoare to suggest to me, for the second time, that a solid front among the newspapers was most desirable. I replied, 'I have taken the King's shilling. I am a King's man.'

Baldwin's approach to Lord Kemsley, Chief of the *Sunday Times* and many other newspapers, was frank and outspoken. He met him at a luncheon given by Lord Fitzalan. Baldwin sought a private conversation with this great newspaper proprietor. He discussed the King's affair and asked Lord Kemsley for his opinion. Lord Kemsley replied that the Non-Conformist Conscience in England was not dead. Baldwin agreed. At the end of the conversation Baldwin said, 'It has been a most interesting talk,' and then added, 'I wish you could take over my task.'[1]

Now, it was natural that he should make a personal approach to Lord Kemsley instead of using an intermediary as in my case. Baldwin held the great newspaper Lord in high esteem, and the Chancellor, Neville Chamberlain, was also intimate with him.

Other newspapers were approached either directly or by intermediary, but these overtures were too numerous to be detailed here. There were also many provincial newspapers which rallied spontaneously to the side of Baldwin without the need of any approach whatever. Faced with this formidable opposition from such a large and influential section of the Press, it was not enough merely to stimulate counter-propaganda in the organs favourable to the King. It was more than ever necessary to remove the marriage issue from public discussion and political decision.

So it happened that even on the day before the storm broke

discussed with them 'The King's matter'. See Lockhart: *Cosmo Gordon Lang*, p. 400.
[1] Information from Lord Kemsley.

in the Press, I was still endeavouring to secure the withdrawal of the whole marriage issue from the Cabinet. I saw Mr. Esmond Harmsworth who told me that he had seen Duff Cooper who was opposed to abdication. Accordingly I saw Duff Cooper. As he was carrying on conversations with the King, I asked him to support my request to His Majesty to withdraw the marriage issue from the Cabinet.

But it was all in vain. On Wednesday, 2nd December, the Cabinet met and reached the decision to oppose the morganatic marriage, come what may. It was also the day on which the *Yorkshire Post* 'belled the cat'. The fight was on and in full public view.

Of course, everything depended on the King's willingness to defend himself. He spoke to me on the night of Wednesday, 2nd December, and told me that he meant to retire into private life. If this statement was final, there was no sense in carrying on the struggle. But I did not believe it was final, for though the King often spoke of abdication he always indicated that he was anxious to remain on the Throne. Whether he made his declaration in a mood of momentary depression or as a half-threat, I did not take it as final, for he had shown that he was most unwilling to leave the Throne and he had taken no practical steps towards abdication. I still believed that he would not abdicate and that he did not want to abdicate.[1]

[1] A day or two after he had spoken to me that Wednesday night he told Lord Brownlow that he did not intend to abdicate but meant to go to Switzerland with Piers Legh, his Equerry, and wait there till the excitement simmered down. Later, when Lord Brownlow was in France, the King said again, this time over the telephone, that he did not mean to abdicate.

VIII

ON THURSDAY, 3rd December, I busied myself in trying to secure a favourable Press for the King. In pursuit of this campaign I saw Sir Walter Layton of the *News Chronicle* for the second time (and I also saw Mr. Churchill and Lord Rothermere). Churchill and I had an interview with Mr. Elias of the *Daily Herald*. He was personally favourable and gave us reason to hope that he would support the King. But his Labour Party colleagues who dictated policy over-ruled Mr. Elias and supported the Abdication.[1]

When the lines of battle were clearly drawn, the newspaper support for the King was certainly more powerful in the country than the opposition. *The Times, Morning Post, Daily Telegraph* and *Daily Herald* were against him and so was the Kemsley Press, but that was only to be expected. On the other hand, the *Express* and the *Mail* Groups were strongly for him, along with some of the provincial papers. We had a powerful propaganda agency at our service, if only we were allowed to use it.[2]

But working for a favourable Press was not my only line of action. It had always been obvious that the King could not possibly withdraw from his intended marriage, but it was

[1] The political policy of the *Daily Herald* was controlled by the Labour Party and the industrial policy by the Trades Union Congress. [Not quite correct. The Labour Party, as such, had no say in regard to the *Daily Herald*. Directors appointed by the Trades Union Congress determined both its political and industrial policy.—Ed.]

[2] Although the London Press did not come out into the open till the next day, 3rd December, I had a very sound idea on Wednesday night as to what line each important paper would take.

doubly impossible once his intention was publicly known. There could be no drawing back on his part, but it was still possible that Mrs. Simpson might withdraw. With this idea in mind I tried to communicate with her. She was living at Fort Belvedere, closely guarded by the King. I drew up a leading article which I thought would be pleasing to her, and I telephoned the King asking permission to read the article to her. He replied by saying that I might send the article to him, and he would show it to her, if he thought fit. He was guarding Mrs. Simpson.

As this method had failed, another had to be tried. The new method was worked out at Stornoway House on the evening of Thursday, 3rd December. On that night Stornoway House seemed to be the centre of everything. There was much coming and going, and much discussion as to the weight of public opinion for and against the King. Mr. Monckton was there and also Mr. Allen, the King's solicitor. It was agreed among us that the best method of persuading Mrs. Simpson was through the agency of someone who had free access to Fort Belvedere. Accordingly, I asked Lord Brownlow to join the consultation (I had already seen him earlier in the day).

When he came I asked him to go next morning, Friday, 4th December, to Fort Belvedere as soon as he knew the King had left for London and try to persuade Mrs. Simpson to make an act of renunciation. This he agreed to do although he knew that it might endanger his friendship with the King.

In the Duke of Windsor's own story he calls this a 'conspiracy'. He uses the word in a good-natured way. But there was no conspiracy. Never at any time did I have a desire to prevent his marriage to Mrs. Simpson. The renunciation I was looking for was never intended to be a final and irrevocable decision. I cannot, of course, speak for the others who were engaged in this scheme, but my sole purpose was to ease the tension and to gain time. If Baldwin were deprived of any excuse for the rush tactics he was so ruthlessly

69

employing, we could enjoy a breathing space and be enabled to present the marriage issue to the public in its true light. With a favourable public opinion supporting him, the King could re-declare his intentions in his own good time and season.

A period of respite for quieter thoughts and for mature consideration had become necessary. The strain of the crisis was telling heavily on the King. He showed it in many ways. He smoked incessantly, sometimes a cigarette, and sometimes a pipe. He kept on saying 'No marriage, no Coronation', repeating this phrase more and more often and with increasing emphasis as the days wore on. Sometimes he would sit with his head in his hands. Occasionally he would wipe the perspiration from his brow with an unfolded handkerchief, or hold the handkerchief against his head, as if to ease some hidden pressure or pain. If he continued to be subjected to this intolerable strain it was clear to me that some rash and fatal and quite unnecessary decision would be taken. Something had to be done to ease the nervous tension, and we considered that an approach to Mrs. Simpson was the most promising means of achieving that end. On Thursday night we decided to make the effort.

Meanwhile, the King was engaged on an effort of his own. He had been working on the draft of a broadcast which he hoped to make to the nation, and on Thursday he sent Mr. Allen to Stornoway House to show the draft to me, asking for my comments and advice, and also asking that I should go over it with Mr. Churchill.

It happened that Churchill was making an important speech in the Albert Hall that night, and he was already preparing to leave his own home for the Hall when Mr. Allen arrived at Stornoway House. Before Churchill made his speech I read the broadcast draft to him on the telephone. He said he would come to Stornoway House after the meeting and discuss the draft. He then made his speech, in which a loyal and friendly reference to the King provoked a storm of applause which showed how deep and widespread was the sympathy of ordinary people for their Monarch in his difficulties.[1]

When he arrived at Stornoway House, we examined the draft and made one or two suggestions to Mr. Allen who was in attendance. For example, we suggested that the word 'Britishers' should be changed to 'British men and women'. We had the intention of making further suggestions if the broadcast was to be delivered, but both of us believed that Baldwin would resist the proposal, claiming in effect that it was an appeal by the King to the people over the heads of the Executive. We united in recommending that the King should read the draft to Baldwin but should on no account give him a copy.·

Friday, 4th December was a day of spectacular ups and downs. Baldwin appeared at a Cabinet meeting with a copy of the draft broadcast which he had obtained somehow or other, against our advice.[2] The Cabinet turned the proposed broadcast down for the very reason which Churchill had anticipated.

The King was therefore silenced, but he found most unexpected spokesmen in Friday morning's Press. It was astonishing that the *Catholic Times*[3] should come out vehemently in favour of the King. No Church is more strongly opposed to divorce than the Catholic Church. But it seemed that even in that communion there were men who might deplore the intended marriage and yet be deeply unwilling to see the Crown made the pawn of politicians.

[1] Popular sympathy with the King was particularly strong among the young. When the Archbishop of Canterbury held a meeting with the leaders of the Free Churches Federation, they told him of this fact, which he heard with dismay. The purpose of the meeting was of course to rally a united religious front against the King.

[2] The Duke of Windsor says in his book that he cannot remember whether he gave Baldwin a copy of the broadcast or not. (*A King's Story*, p. 365.)

[3] In 1936 the Editor of the *Catholic Times* was a well-known priest, Father Bernard Grimley.

71

But, far more encouraging for us, and far more shattering for Baldwin, was the attitude of the *News Chronicle*. This newspaper was the traditional though unofficial voice of the Non-Conformist Conscience.[1] If Baldwin had reason to expect total support anywhere it was in this quarter. But the *News Chronicle* came out with a bold and stimulating advocacy of the morganatic marriage. Baldwin might well feel that he had been 'wounded in the house of a friend'. Indeed, the public response to the proposal was so enthusiastic that he may have felt that he was worse than wounded. Politically, he was in immediate danger of being killed stone dead. There appeared to be a tide now running with immense and gathering force in favour of the King. If the hearts of the King's supporters were uplifted there was good reason for it.

Very soon there was even better reason for optimism. Our plan for getting Lord Brownlow to put the case for renunciation to Mrs. Simpson looked like being entirely defeated by the simple fact that the King did not leave the Fort for London on that Friday (4th December). So long as he was in the Fort there was no possibility of making a private approach to Mrs. Simpson. But the King himself gave us an opportunity far better than we had dared to hope for. He decided that Mrs. Simpson must go to France for her own peace of mind, and the man he chose to accompany her was none other than Lord Brownlow. We relied upon him to press the case for renunciation as soon as the journey started and he did not fail us.[2]

[1] Baldwin in his speeches sometimes claimed association with the Non-Conformists and rightly. His father was a Methodist and his mother was the daughter of an eminent Methodist preacher. When his migration to the Church of England took place is unknown to me. It is quite common, however, for politicians to claim advantages from association with Non-Conformity and also the Episcopacy. [Baldwin's parents in fact moved over to the Church of England before he was born.—Ed.]

[2] When Lord Brownlow was driving Mrs. Simpson to Newhaven, en route he proposed that she should abandon the trip and take refuge, in hiding, at his own house of Belton near Grantham. But she refused and

72

If our hopes were high, there was good reason. With the Press support that the King enjoyed, it now seemed possible to swing the country in favour of him and against Baldwin. Baldwin was subjected to a flank attack from the *News Chronicle* that was gathering frightening speed and momentum, and the powerful *Mail* and *Express* groups were geared for action in defence of the King. If public opinion could be brought round to the King's side, and if Mrs. Simpson would agree to offer a withdrawal from the marriage, Baldwin would find that his seemingly impregnable position had been overturned. The future was bright with promise. Victory seemed to be within our grasp.

the journey to France continued. Lord Brownlow's reason for this suggestion was his conviction that the absence of Mrs. Simpson in a foreign land would increase the King's agitation. I had thought otherwise, but Lord Brownlow proved to be right.

IX

THEN CAME a crushing blow. On Thursday, when all seemed so fair, I was informed that Mr. Monckton could not see me any more. He was engaging on negotiations with the Government on the terms of abdication and must disassociate himself from those who were in the other camp. He did not wish to endanger the financial conditions of abdication by maintaining contacts of which Baldwin disapproved. For the first time I believed that the King was seriously determined to abdicate. He had taken the first practical step towards the surrender of his Throne and from that step he would find it difficult to draw back.

But I was not yet ready to give up the cause as lost. On Friday, I wrote to Monckton asking him to keep open some channel of communication with me, and informing him in effect that as long as the King remained on the Throne there was no danger from intervention in the Simpson divorce case. This, I understood, was the verdict of the Law Advisers, and it was important that the King should be fortified by the assurance. He needed all the ammunition he could get. I wrote as follows:

December 4, 1936.

My dear Monckton,

Brownlow told me yesterday that you wanted to keep free of me on account of your desire to sustain your relations with Mr. Baldwin and the other Ministers.

I sympathize very deeply with that view and I understand altogether the reasons which dictate your decision.

But I hope the ban does not apply to telephone communications and to letters discreetly and properly framed, because there is much that I would like to say to you. But if you prefer that communications should be cut off altogether, I hope you will indicate some other person so that I may still have a medium for sending my observations to His Majesty. For, of course, I do not want to interrupt and interfere with His Majesty continually by putting in telephone calls, or sending letters either, for that matter.

Now my present concern is to inform you, and, of course, His Majesty, of a conversation that took place last night (Thursday) between O'Connor[1] and Harmsworth. I am authorised by Harmsworth to give you a record of it.

O'Connor said that if the King remained on his Throne, the King's Proctor or any private complainant would in law find it impossible to raise objections to the progress of the divorce case. He stated that there were positive legal objections to any such course. He said, further, that if the King did not remain on his Throne it would be possible for the law officer or the intervenor to interfere with the hearing of the case.

Now I know there is not any obstacle to the due process of the law resulting in a verdict for the plaintiff but I am certain that ill-disposed persons and others seeking notoriety intend to try to intervene. So I hope very much that this information will be taken into account by you and any others who may be concerned with advising the King.

I understood Harmsworth to say that the opinion put forward by O'Connor represented the combined judgment of the Law Officers.

Yours sincerely,

On that same Friday, I had lunch with Sir Samuel Hoare. I mentioned to him as many favourable items as I could

[1] The Solicitor-General.

muster which might help the King's cause, and also the immense strength the King had gained from the support of so large and influential a section of the Press. I expressed hopes too that the crisis might yet be solved by an act of renunciation on the part of Mrs. Simpson.

There were such promising events in the King's favour. If only Hoare could be convinced that the King would continue in the seat of power, I hoped he might take a greater interest in the cause of His Majesty. For after all, the King's authority flowed from the fact that responsibility devolved on him for calling the next Prime Minister, should Baldwin go. Hoare was a likely selection, but the King could, if he chose, send for someone else. Unhappily, Hoare was not receptive to my arguments and remained unmoved by my advocacy.

Accordingly I asked Mr. Allen, the King's solicitor, to deliver to the King a copy of the letter I had addressed to Mr. Monckton, and intended, of course, for His Majesty himself. As there were to be no more talks with me, I might as well use two lines of communication for this final message. But the King rejected my request for an interview. He repeated Mr. Monckton's representations that there was nothing left to settle but the terms of abdication, and in such negotiations I could be of no help. I would be a hindrance.

Friday was also a day of action for Mr. Baldwin. He was becoming impatient of delay. Although I was excluded from further conversations with the King—and Mr. Baldwin was within his constitutional rights in deciding to reject me—our Prime Minister now admitted Mr. Churchill to the councils of the Sovereign. So it was a Good Friday for Churchill who was being consulted directly for the first time, and a Bad Friday for me since I was tossed out of the Council Chamber.

However, I was told on behalf of the King that I could talk with Churchill who was going to the Fort at seven o'clock. With that I had to be content. Thus our roles were reversed. Churchill had relied on me for a line of communication. Now I must depend on him.

Churchill went to the Fort for dinner and urged the King not to abdicate. He insisted that there was no constitutional issue at stake and there could be none until marriage became a practical possibility. He was angry with Baldwin for securing the promise of the Opposition not to form an alternative Government. He insisted on the importance of delay. He raised the whole controversy to the high level of the hereditary principle[1], and he asked the King to demand a release from strain, on the advice of his doctors, and then to retire to Windsor, to pull up the drawbridge and refuse to parley.

Churchill drove straight from the Fort to my house. It was the King himself who telephoned me to advise me of Churchill's coming. Hope flared up again for the last time, for this was restoration of communications. When the King had refused to see me on this very same day I concluded that he did indeed intend to abdicate. When he spoke to me on the telephone that Friday night, I also concluded that he had changed his mind and was ready to fight for his Throne after all. Churchill was of the same mind. His vigour, eloquence and enthusiasm appeared to have put fresh heart into the King. When Churchill arrived at Stornoway House at two in the morning he told me that he meant to write two letters, one to the King himself, and one to the Prime Minister. He was also preparing a statement for the Press.

When he left me at a late hour my spirits had recovered from the earlier shock of the King's intimation that he meant

[1] 'Whatever else might happen, he [Churchill] argued, the hereditary principle must not be left to the mercy of politicians trimming their doctrines "to the varying hour".' (*A King's Story*, p. 382.)

I held similar views. On 11th December, 1936, I wrote to a friend in Canada: 'For abdication is a very grave course. While it may close one set of problems, it opens another. For instance, it is an object lesson in the quick disposal of a monarch, who got at cross-purposes with the executive. And later on, other and different executives may profit by the lesson. For the truth is, that much of the stability of the Throne is derived from the fact that it has been stable.'

to abdicate. Churchill's enthusiasm was infectious and I felt I had good reason to believe that the King had reversed his fatal decision. I was further strengthened by yet another piece of good news.

A message in code had come from France. It was a simple code, using the names of members of my family to suggest that the message was meant for me, whereas it was meant for transmission to the King. It was impossible to mistake the meaning of this message. Mrs. Simpson was willing to withdraw from the marriage.[1]

Adding up the happy and unhappy events of the day, the balance appeared to be healthy. The King was once more in the field, or so I believed. He had a wider and more influential support in the Press than we ever anticipated. He had the immense support of Churchill[2]—and Mrs. Simpson's withdrawal might well create a dramatic change in the whole situation.

Here, it seemed, was a last chance. If the Churchill policy was followed, and if the renunciation was heavily emphasized, there was every hope that the day might yet be won.

But the Churchill policy was not followed, and the golden opportunity offered by the renunciation was entirely lost. The responsibility was the King's. Throughout all the days of public controversy he shackled the Press that was favourable to himself. He would allow us no liberty in expressing our views or in arguing strongly for his cause. His chief desire was to secure a minimum of publicity for Mrs. Simp-

[1] Here is the code message: 'W. M. Janet strongly advising the James Company to postpone purchase of Chester shares to next autumn and to announce decision by verbal methods, thereby increasing popularity, maintaining prestige, but also the right to re-open negotiations by the autumn.' (The Duke of Windsor reveals the code for telegrams. Beaverbrook was Tornado; Baldwin Crutch; Churchill W.S.C., and the King Mr. James after St. James's Palace (*A King's Story*, p. 376).)

[2] From the Lloyd George Papers I learn that Churchill shouted to Baldwin across the floor of the House: 'You won't be satisfied until you've broken him, will you?' This remark was not, however, recorded in *Hansard* or the newspapers.

son. He was also anxious to avoid any suggestion of conflict with Baldwin. As a result, the pro-Baldwin Press had the field all to itself. The Press attacked the King with increasing bitterness right to the end of the crisis and even beyond, while the newspapers favourable to the King were crippled in everything they sought to do. There could be only one end to a contest waged on such terms.

But, by Saturday, 5th December, the King's errors of policy had ceased to matter, and my last hope was totally extinguished. For on that very morning the King said to Walter Monckton, 'I want you to go to London and tell the Prime Minister that when he comes to see me this afternoon, I shall formally tell him that I have decided to abdicate.'

Walter Monckton duly performed this melancholy errand.

A member of the Cabinet[1] came to my house and told me the news. It was evident to me that Mr. Baldwin intended that I should be persuaded by this revelation to cease from further agitation. Now Sir Samuel Hoare was Mr. Baldwin's intermediary with me. It was curious that another should have given me the information. Hoare, however, sent me a letter a few days later. He declared that now an irrevocable decision had been taken there was nothing more for him to do. He wrote: 'I tried my best to the end to make renunciation possible, but the King would not move an inch.'[2]

Several Members of Parliament and Newspaper Editors had also been given the news of the King's intention and in the constituencies word was circulating that the struggle between King and Prime Minister was over, with victory perching on the banners of Baldwin. Further controversy, it was explained, should be stilled.

Unfortunately, the same information was not conveyed to Churchill. Like myself, he had thought on Friday night that

[1] [The member of the Cabinet was Sir John Simon.—Ed.]
[2] See *Sunday Dispatch*, 7th October, 1951, Lord Templewood (Sir Samuel Hoare) on the Abdication. [Templewood wrongly dated the letter in his *Sunday Dispatch* article. It was in fact written on 10th December.—Ed.]

the King had decided to resist abdication after all. But, unlike myself, he still thought the same on Saturday. I went to his Westminster flat at eleven o'clock on that morning. He read me his statement to the Press. It was a most moving and most powerful document but I knew that it was now too late. I said 'Our cock won't fight,' and told him I believed that the King's decision was absolute and final, and that any further struggles to save him would do no good.

On the previous night Churchill's eloquence had made a momentary impression on the King, but it was only momentary. Churchill was now flogging a dead horse, but I could not convince him of the fact. I left him with the parting words, 'No dice,' but he would not believe my miserable news.

But while the King had committed himself to Abdication, the events of Saturday afternoon were to cast strange shades and contours on the crisis. In yielding to Baldwin's demand for immediate action, the King had asked a corresponding favour from his Prime Minister. On Saturday, 5th December, His Majesty suggested that the Bill of Abdication should be accompanied by a second Bill to make Mrs. Simpson's divorce absolute at once.[1] Baldwin consented. He went further. He promised his own resignation should he fail to implement the legislation.[2]

But he counted without his colleagues. On Sunday, the proposed marriage Bill met with strong opposition from some of the most influential Cabinet members.

Inskip, speaking for the 'Low' Church element, said that the Church simply could not tolerate what was in effect a Bill facilitating re-marriage for a divorced person. Such toleration would undermine the very foundations of the Church. And what the Church could not tolerate, Inskip would not tolerate. Halifax spoke for the 'High' Church which regards

[1] See *A King's Story*, p. 387.
[2] See *A King's Story*, p. 391. ' "Sir," he assured me, "I shall resign if the Cabinet refuses you the second Bill." '

divorce as an abomination. Kingsley Wood, a Methodist, said that the Bill would lose votes.

Sunday was therefore a dreadful day for the 'self-interested manipulator'. His Divorce Bill was rejected. He could not carry his own Cabinet. He dared not face the opposition of his colleagues. What then?

The exceedingly agile Prime Minister was in a very difficult situation. But not for long. He had promised resignation if the 'Divorce Bill' failed. Would he resign? No; a thousand times No. He would try another expedient. Mrs. Simpson had made a statement to the Press declaring she was willing to withdraw from the unhappy situation.[1] Could Baldwin not pin her down to declare that she would withdraw her divorce proceedings? Thus the need for the Divorce Bill would be disposed of and Baldwin could escape from his dilemma.

Mr. Goddard, Mrs. Simpson's solicitor, was invited to visit Mr. Baldwin at Downing Street. He was asked to go to Cannes. Accordingly he left by Government aeroplane, arriving on Tuesday night, 9th December. Goddard's heart was troubling him and this was his first flight. He was therefore accompanied by his physician Dr. Kirkwood, who was mistakenly described as a gynaecologist.[2] A lawyer's clerk made up the party.[3]

Excitement flared, and rumours distressing to the King

[1] The full text will be found on p. 106.

[2] On 10th December, Dr. Kirkwood declared he was not a gynaecologist and insisted he was only a general physician (*Daily Mail*, 10th December, 1936).

Dr. William Kirkwood was in fact a Clinical Assistant with a resident job for a short time at Queen Charlotte's Maternity Hospital. He was a House Surgeon at St. George's Hospital. He was not classed as a gynaecologist. He was in general practice with an interest in disorders peculiar to women. Being at Queen Charlotte's was all part of his general training.

[3] Newspapers described the clerk as an anaesthetist. Lord Brownlow, referring to the Goddard incident, declared that he was absolutely horrified, hurt and deeply angered that this ridiculous story should have got into circulation.

and Mrs. Simpson were retold throughout the country. The Press printed restrained but damaging reports. American newspapers pounced on such exciting and absorbing material.

When Mr. Goddard interviewed Mrs. Simpson on Wednesday morning, 9th December, she was evasive and indefinite in her conversation. She may have guessed the motives of our ingenious Prime Minister in sending Goddard to see her.[1]

Would Mrs. Simpson save Baldwin from fulfilling his pledge of resignation by cancelling her divorce proceedings against Mr. Simpson, which was within her legal rights? Would she pull him out of his deep well of deception and deceit? No.

The game was up. Baldwin failed. His emissary had asked the direct question. 'Was it wise to continue with the divorce proceedings and to obtain the decree absolute?' This plea was rejected. Baldwin then broke his pledge without hesitation or explanation—a pledge solemnly given to his own Sovereign. Guilty Prime Minister.

On Tuesday, 8th December, there was another amazing development. Sir John Simon, Secretary of State for Home Affairs, and eminent counsel, had given an opinion to the Prime Minister on 3rd December, that intervention in the Simpson divorce case by the King's Proctor could not be maintained. On Tuesday, 8th December, he changed his mind. Intervention by the King's Proctor, said Sir John, might now be necessary if private persons attempted to stop the divorce decree becoming absolute. Abdication, he declared, would not improve the hope of marriage between Mrs. Simpson and the King.

It was on this day that Mr. Francis Stephenson, a lawyer's clerk, filed an affidavit in support of an application to the King's Proctor. Stephenson did not take further action and

[1] Goddard's statement of his mission to Cannes is printed in Appendix C. Authority for publication was given to me in writing.

the Attorney-General, Sir Donald Somervell, asked for a withdrawal of the petition.[1]

The King had been told on Sunday that the Divorce Bill had been rejected. On Tuesday he was given a copy of Sir John Simon's formidable letter relating to the King's Proctor. By now his anxieties were overwhelming, and Baldwin appeared to be his only sure passage to the haven of marriage. The Prime Minister had not only 'collared the martyrdom' but he had also crushed the spirit of his King.[2]

Baldwin was the master of the departing monarch who dared not speak a word of complaint. Marriage was now his only goal.

On Wednesday, 9th December, the general public learned what the Cabinet and many others had known since Saturday, the 5th, that Abdication was decided. On Thursday, the 10th, Baldwin made his Abdication statement to the Commons, and on Friday, 11th December, the King gave his Royal Assent to the Act which ended his own reign.

But, in fact, that reign had ended on Saturday, 5th December, 1936. The intervening days were filled with noisy, but useless, controversy in public and in private, with the handling of the formalities and details of what had already been decided beyond all hope of recall.

[1] Sir Boyd Merriman asked the King's Proctor to examine Mr. Stephenson's intervention on 19th January, 1937. The motion for withdrawal of the petition was granted on 19th March.

[2] The King wrote of the crushing news of the failure of the Divorce Bill that he 'had to stand silent'. He was lonely in his unequal contest with the Prime Minister. He was aware that his friends in Parliament dared not speak in his defence, lest they should lose party favour. See *A King's Story*, p. 394.

X

THE SEPARATION of the King's private fortune from the Royal Estate involved tedious and difficult negotiations and several days were given over to discussions.

He owned Balmoral and Sandringham outright. The contents of Buckingham Palace belonged to him subject to entail. It was planned to transfer these properties to the Royal Establishment.

The deed was done. By Thursday, 10th December, the Throne was passing to another and the King was preparing for exile. It was then that Baldwin rose in the Commons to tell the story of the Crisis.

He spoke to the same House which had listened to him in shocked dismay less than a month before, when he confessed that he had misled the nation on the need for rearmament. But this time he was total master of the situation.

When he began to speak he already commanded the approval of the House. When he ended, he could count on the respect and confidence and even the admiration of nearly every Member.

The speech was a masterpiece. There was no attempt at

rhetoric, which Baldwin always affected to despise. There was no evidence of laborious preparation. He spoke from a few notes which he held in his hand (the same hand that held the Deed of Abdication). He was informal, almost colloquial. He blamed nobody, nor did he seek to praise himself. He merely told a simple tale, with every appearance of candour. The speech was utterly unadorned and surprisingly short for the greatness of the occasion, but Baldwin succeeded in creating the impression he wanted to create in the minds of his hearers and of the millions who read him in the newspapers.

By skilful, subtle and unnoticed touches, he painted a picture of himself. It was the picture of a loyal, honest and humble English gentleman who had striven to serve his King and had suffered much in his strivings. He let it be inferred that the difficulties were created by the King, and by the King alone. Baldwin had done his earnest best to solve them. He had tried to save the King from himself. It was a bitter disappointment that he had failed, but where he failed no one else could have succeeded. All was done that man could do. And if he had failed to save the King, he had succeeded at least in saving the Monarchy.

He claimed that he sought to serve the King not only out of duty as his principal servant but also as his devoted friend. There was confidence between King and Prime Minister. More than that, there was positive affection. The King wanted no one but Baldwin to assist him in his agonizing decision, and the lamentable end of the crisis had left the friendship not only unimpaired, but stronger. Like every other subject in the land, Baldwin had lost a King, but he had cemented a friendship that would last for life. The good and faithful servant made it clear that he had done his duty to the limits of his endurance in a spirit of self-sacrifice, without counting the cost to himself. No one who heard him and fully believed him could doubt that he deserved well of his King and country.

It was deeply moving. It was utterly convincing. It was also utterly untrue.

I had watched the course of events with close attention, and I read Baldwin's speech with no surprise. It was impossible to deny admiration to the speech as a piece of special pleading. It was a perfect example of the art which conceals art. But it was also a perfect example of unscrupulous advocacy. I had long known Mr. Baldwin's lack of sincerity and candour, but I was startled by the depths of his disingenuousness on this occasion. I thought it a tragedy that the King should have gone, but no less a tragedy that a man so deeply steeped in political cunning should be restored to unchallenged supremacy to govern, or misgovern, the country.

If a man wishes to mislead and deceive his hearers, he need not be driven to the telling of a direct and simple lie.[1] He can achieve the same effect by using the suggestion of the false and the suppression of the true. These were the means that Baldwin employed. He managed to suggest that at all times he was deeply anxious to save the King on his Throne. But I knew that as his own position was threatened, he was determined to drive the King off the Throne. But suggestion of the false was less important than suppression of the truth. I was one of several persons who were intimately concerned in the King's tragedy, on the King's side, and I knew how much Baldwin did not tell the House of Commons.

(1) He did not tell the House that within a few days of the death of King George V, Baldwin had learned from 'the surest sources that the new King intended to marry Mrs. Simpson'.[2]

King George V died on 20th January, but it was not until

[1] There was one lie. Baldwin stated that 'This is the first and last occasion on which I was the one who asked for an interview (with the King).' He asked for two interviews, on the 20th of October and on the 8th of December.

[2] See Templewood: *Nine Troubled Years*, p. 215.

20th October that Baldwin raised the matter, and even then raised it in a half-hearted and inconclusive way. For more than eight months he allowed the King to commit himself irrevocably to the marriage project without giving him the slightest hint that the marriage would be opposed with all the forces at Baldwin's command. For more than eight months he allowed the King to become enmeshed in his plans for marriage. Even when the proposal became the subject of flaring headlines in the American Press, Baldwin still gave no indication of his secret knowledge, or of the plans he was preparing to thwart the King's dearest wish, or to drive him from the Throne. Worse still, he accepted the King's hospitality, dining with him in the company of Mrs. Simpson, exchanging the courtesies of social life with the lady and showing the normal friendliness that such an occasion demands. And all the time he was lying in wait to destroy the King or wreck the happiness of Mrs. Simpson. Not until 16th November did the King tell Baldwin that he meant to marry.

(2) He did not tell the House that he secured the support of the Opposition Parties before he spoke to the King about his marriage intentions. He had also made efforts to secure a unanimous Press in his favour.[1]

(3) He did not tell the House that he had discussed the procedure of Abdication with colleagues before he even mentioned Abdication at all to the King.[2]

(4) He did not tell the House that he had given the King's Private Secretary the information which formed the basis of his ominous letter which forced the King to declare his intentions.[3]

(5) He did not tell the House that the bitterly hostile editor of *The Times* had been consulted on the draft of this

[1] See letter from Sir Archibald Sinclair, p. 58, the Hardinge letter to the King; Lockhart: *Cosmo Gordon Lang*, p. 400.
[2] See Hardinge letter and *A King's Story*, p. 326.
[3] See *History of The Times*, Vol. 4, part II, p. 1030, and Hardinge: *Before the Abdication* (*The Times*, 29th November, 1955).

letter and had approved of sending it to the King as a 'courageous' document.[1]

(6) There was no mention of the refusal to allow the King to go for a short stay in Belgium or Switzerland, to ease his own mind and to let public excitement cool.[2]

(7) There was no mention of the withholding from the King of the Cabinet papers concerning the marriage, in defiance of all precedent and also in defiance of his simple duty.[3]

(8) He never mentioned his refusal of the King's request to broadcast.[4]

(9) He did not tell the House that he himself had framed the reference to the Dominions, had not shown it to the King and had not shown him the answers, except one that was most unfavourable.[5]

(10) He did not give any account of the first New Zealand answer which was not satisfactory to himself, nor did he mention the approach to a New Zealand Minister to ensure that the final answer would be what he required.[6]

(11) He did not tell the House that when the King asked that the whole marriage issue should be withdrawn from the consideration of the home and the Dominions Cabinets, he simply ignored the request.[7]

(12) On Friday, 4th December, Baldwin asked the King to decide on the spot about Abdication, and failing an immediate answer, he demanded a decision before the week-end was up. He never mentioned it in Parliament.[8]

(13) He did not disclose that the day before receiving con-

---

[1] See *History of The Times*, Vol. 4, part II, p. 1030; Wrench: *Geoffrey Dawson and Our Times*, p. 345, and Hardinge: *Before the Abdication*.

[2] See *A King's Story*, p. 361.   [3] See *A King's Story*, p. 346.

[4] See *A King's Story*, pp. 378–9, and Templewood: *Nine Troubled Years*, p. 221.

[5] See this narrative, Chapter Six, also Lockhart's *Cosmo Gordon Lang*, p. 402.

[6] See p. 62.   [7] See my conversation with Mr. Monckton, p. 65.

[8] See *A King's Story*, p. 379.

sent to Abdication, the Duke of York (George VI) was notified of his Kingship.[1]

(14) When he did get the King's decision on Saturday, 5th December, he promised to do something for the King, in return for his speedy Abdication. He promised to bring in a Parliamentary Bill to make Mrs. Simpson's divorce absolute at once, so that her marriage to the King could be immediate. No more tempting bribe could have been offered to the King, and Baldwin went so far as to say that if he failed to carry the Bill, he would resign.[2] He did not tell this to the House, nor did he say that within twenty-four hours, one cock-crow, he broke that promise.

(15) The broken promise created difficulties on Sunday, 6th December. When Walter Monckton, the King's adviser, was told that there would be no Divorce Bill, he said that the King would need time to reconsider his position. At once all forms of pressure were applied by Baldwin and his colleagues. There were threats of damage to the Christmas shopping trade, threats of a Stock Exchange panic, threats of unemployment. Baldwin summed up by saying that the matter must be settled by Christmas. The story of this severe pressure was concealed.[3]

(16) On Tuesday night, 8th December, Baldwin said, 'Only time I was frightened. I thought he (the King) might change his mind.' In the morning, 9th December, the same Baldwin sent a letter to the King asking him to change his mind.[4]

What he neglected to tell was the story which provided the true explanation of his conduct and his policy. What he did tell was no more than a recital of the empty and insincere gestures he had made. While professing to serve the King he had worked to destroy him. The picture he painted was as false as it was fair, but it was believed.

[1] Young: *Stanley Baldwin*, p. 241.   [2] *A King's Story*, p. 391.
[3] See Mr. Monckton's account, recorded in *A King's Story*, pp. 392–3.
[4] See G. M. Young: *Stanley Baldwin*, p. 243.

A final touch of meanness was being added even while Baldwin was speaking. The King had asked him to insert two messages into his address to Parliament. One was a reference to the Duke of York who was to ascend the Throne. The other was a reference to Mrs. Simpson explaining that she had always sought to avoid abdication.[1] We have since learned that the omission of Mrs. Simpson's name was deliberate and the reason was that Baldwin regarded her with contempt and he would not do her justice, even when the struggle was over.[2]

On the following night the King spoke. Half the world was listening but I had a special reason for paying close attention, for the speech was based on the original draft for the broadcast which Baldwin had refused to sanction. Mr. George Allen had brought that draft to me at Stornoway House and I had gone over it with care.

Of course, there were inevitably a good many changes to meet the changed circumstances. The King was no longer speaking to defend his Throne but explaining why he had felt impelled to surrender it. But of these changes I knew nothing. Since communications had been cut off, I knew no more than any other citizen about the King's affairs. Therefore I was specially anxious to know what the King would now have to say.

I listened to the speech in my home at Cherkley with a few friends. I was delighted and fascinated by the quality of the delivery and the rhythm of the King's voice. I was also deeply moved, as so many millions were, by the dignity, the

[1] When Mrs. Simpson reached Cannes she went with Lord Brownlow to visit Mr. Esmond Harmsworth. On the way back from the visit Mrs. Simpson decided to issue a statement to the Press, declaring that she was abandoning the marriage and would leave Europe for the United States, via Genoa, for an indefinite period. Lord Brownlow drafted the statement and Mrs. Simpson signed it. But Lord Brownlow felt it his duty to advise Mrs. Simpson to read the statement by telephone to the King before Lord Brownlow issued it to the Press. She did so, and the King objected so strongly that it was never issued.
[2] See *The Times Literary Supplement*, 28th September, 1951.

absence of rancour and the deep sincerity of the utterance. I was listening with the greatest admiration and pleasure when suddenly I was startled to hear the King speak of Baldwin in terms of friendship. I could not believe that I had heard rightly. I knew how Baldwin had treated the King and I knew what the King really thought of Baldwin's behaviour towards himself. I knew because he had told me. For that reason I could not understand this complimentary phrase, and I continued to be puzzled until the King revealed the secret in his own story. Baldwin had asked him for this friendly reference, and he had agreed to make it.[1]

Apart from this seemingly inexplicable compliment, the speech was a masterpiece, of a different kind from Baldwin's, but equally effective in doing all that a speech could do. Baldwin had made himself out to be the great sufferer, the one who had endured in patient silence. In the words of H. G. Wells, he had 'collared the martyrdom'. The parting message of the Duke of Windsor did something to correct that illusion. It reminded people that it was the King who had lost his Throne, while the Prime Minister remained in office.

It was easy to recognize the accent of sincerity in the King's farewell. In millions of homes there were second thoughts on the Abdication and perhaps some degree of compunction. The Duke of Windsor by one masterly speech had recaptured public sympathy and had even won a great

[1] No wonder the King consented to say words in praise of Baldwin. His future happiness depended on marriage with Mrs. Simpson. And marriage with Mrs. Simpson, the King knew quite well, now depended on Mr. Baldwin. The Duke took a very different view when he came to write his own story. By that time the marriage lines had been spoken at Tours. His dearly loved fiancée was now his cherished partner 'for good or for ill, until death do them part'. Of Baldwin he wrote then: 'Yet my own recollection of the same occasion, constant through the years, is not so much that of a generous Prime Minister trying to help his Sovereign through a personal situation of almost indescribable complexity as that of a political Procrustes determined to fit his regal victim into the iron bed of convention' (*A King's Story*, p. 317).

deal of admiration. In foreign cities thousands of miles away women wept openly in the street. It was a triumph of natural and sincere eloquence. It won back the people's good will. But it could not win back the Throne. That was gone for ever.

The discredited and ridiculed Prime Minister had been the victor. The much-loved and greatly praised hereditary Monarch had been dethroned.

But there was yet another speech to be delivered, a parting word by the Archbishop of Canterbury. As he had kept a discreet and determined silence so long as the Crisis was raging, it might have been thought that he would continue his silence when the Crisis was past and nothing that anyone said could have any practical effect. But the Archbishop thought differently. On Sunday, 13th December, he addressed the nation by wireless. It was not a speech of farewell but of outright condemnation.

The ex-King, he said, had sought his happiness in a manner inconsistent with Christian principles, and within a social circle whose standards of life were alien to all the best instincts and traditions of his people. Those who belonged to this circle stood rebuked by the nation which had loved King Edward.[1]

[1] This allegation by the Archbishop threatened to have unfortunate repercussions for himself. Lord Brownlow considered that he was one of the King's friends who had been publicly attacked, and he was advised that he had grounds for an action for damages. Accordingly he asked for a meeting with the Archbishop.

When he was seeing Baldwin at Chequers, the subject of his intended suit against the Archbishop arose, and Baldwin said that he never interfered in Church affairs. But he did interfere, in a characteristically devious way.

For Lord Brownlow was hardly back in London before he was approached by Sir Philip Game, Commissioner of Police, who asked him to call on Sir John Simon, the Home Secretary. Sir John Simon, in the course of conversation, gave Lord Brownlow an assurance that telephones were not tapped in Britain (Lord Brownlow had voiced suspicions on this point). Sir John then asked Lord Brownlow if he was going to see the Archbishop, and when Lord Brownlow said he was, Sir John tried to dissuade him. He even offered to cancel the appointment himself, then

The speech provoked a storm of angry protest. Even those who had supported Baldwin throughout were scandalized by this vitriolic outburst. Letters poured into Lambeth Palace denouncing the Archbishop. Even Lang's official biographer, Mr. J. G. Lockhart, cannot defend the speech. He says that the Archbishop was 'overpowered' by his sense of pathos and contrast. Others thought he was overpowered with bitterness and uncharity.

However, the Archbishop had one staunch defender who praised him warmly without reserve or qualification. That was Stanley Baldwin. Three days before the scandalous broadcast, Baldwin in the Commons had publicly proclaimed his friendship with the ex-King, a friendship which he said had been cemented for life. And then the same man wrote in his own hand a letter of enthusiastic congratulations to the author of the venomous attack on the man he claimed as friend.[1] He told the Archbishop that his speech was the voice of Christian England.

In the whole sorry record of Baldwin's duplicity and dishonesty, there is no episode more contemptible than this.

The depth of his hypocrisy was revealed with equal clarity in a conversation he held with Lord Brownlow after his return from France. Lord Brownlow discussed his efforts to secure a really effective renunciation from Mrs. Simpson. Baldwin said, 'If you had succeeded, I would have put you in the Tower for life.' In the same talk Baldwin compared

and there, by telephone. But Lord Brownlow refused to let the matter drop so easily.

He called at Lambeth Palace. He was rather surprised when the butler urged him to be very quiet, and he asked the reason. The butler explained that silence was necessary because His Grace might be at prayer. But His Grace was not at prayer. He was quite otherwise engaged. Lord Brownlow found him sitting at a large desk which was covered with cuttings from American newspapers referring to his broadcast. He was unwilling to give Lord Brownlow a written statement but he assured him that no attack on his character had been intended and authorized him to repeat this assurance wherever and whenever he thought fit. With this verbal apology Lord Brownlow was content.

[1] Lockhart: *Cosmo Gordon Lang*, p. 405.

93

himself to Cromwell. This was hardly fair to the Great Protector. After all, Cromwell never pretended that his only desire was to keep Charles the First on the Throne or that Charles regarded him with affection and trust.[1]

[1] The last meeting between the King and Baldwin took place on the evening of Tuesday, 8th December (after Abdication had been decided). Baldwin asked for it. Before leaving London for the Fort to have 'deep speech' with the King, he said to his secretaries, 'He (the King) must wrestle with himself now in a way he has never done before, and if he will let me, I will help him. We may even have to see the night through together.' (See Young: *Stanley Baldwin*, p. 243, and *A King's Story*, p. 401.)

Baldwin went to Fort Belvedere armed with a bag, meaning to spend the night. But his design went wrong, for the King let him know that he would not be invited to stay, and, during the whole meeting, the Abdication was not mentioned at all. Baldwin left the Fort at half-past nine. Thus, his Elmer Gantry effort was a failure.

But why did he make the effort? What was his purpose? He was seeking to collect material for his Commons speech, in which he meant to picture himself as the devoted and faithful servant who struggled to the last to save the soul of a wayward master and who had even spent a night-long vigil in a last endeavour to bring that master to the mercy seat. But he did not collect the material. The King foiled his purpose, the only purpose he had in making the visit. In writing after the Abdication, the Duke of Windsor said: '... I had already had quite enough of Mr. Baldwin; his part in my life was over, and I did not propose to have him on my hands that night, snapping his fingers, storing up little homely touches for his report to Parliament' (*A King's Story*, p. 401).

A LOYALIST AT PRAYER

MRS. SIMPSON IN THE SOUTH OF FRANCE

9 . 12 . 36
8 pm

THE FORT,
SUNNINGDALE, ASCOT.

The only conditions on
which I can stay here, are
if I renounce you for
all time.

THE KING TO MRS. SIMPSON

INSTRUMENT OF ABDICATION

I, Edward the Eighth, of Great Britain, Ireland, and the British Dominions beyond the Seas, King, Emperor of India, do hereby declare My irrevocable determination to renounce the Throne for Myself and for My descendants, and My desire that effect should be given to this Instrument of Abdication immediately.

In token whereof I have hereunto set My hand this tenth day of December, nineteen hundred and thirty six, in the presence of the witnesses whose signatures are subscribed.

SIGNED AT
FORT BELVEDERE
IN THE PRESENCE
OF

Edward RI

Albert

Henry.

George.

THE INSTRUMENT OF ABDICATION

THE SUCCESSOR

MARRIED AT LAST

HONEYMOON WITH DOG

HAPPILY EVER AFTER

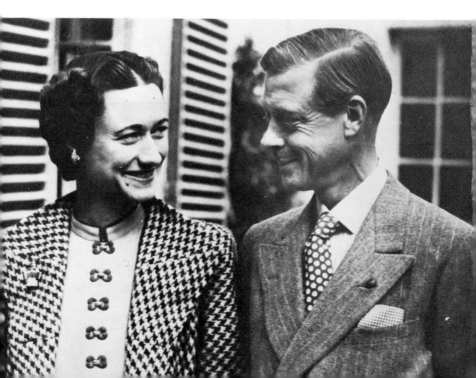

XI

SEVERAL TIMES in my life I have been intimately concerned in important political contests and upheavals and I
have discovered that there is always an important character
working behind the scenes, a man whose activities are unnoticed by the public but who exercises a great effect on the
course of events. This was certainly true of the Abdication
Crisis. The man behind the scenes was Geoffrey Dawson,
editor of *The Times*. He was Baldwin's intimate adviser and
he did much to make the Abdication a certainty.

I came across Geoffrey Dawson fairly frequently during
the first World War. He had a keen interest in the latest
political developments. He was quite often to be seen in the
outer offices of Whitehall, waiting for the chance of 'a word'
with some Minister who could give him useful information
concerning politics.

He dined regularly at a well-known dining club of political,
legal and ecclesiastical leaders.[1] He was an animated conver-
sationalist and was quick to grasp implications and tendencies
concerning policies and personalities. He was a dapper little
man, with a pleasant manner.

His most intimate friend in political circles was Baldwin.
They met each other constantly, were members of the same
club and served together on the Rhodes Trust.

Dawson's original name was Robinson. He made the
change of name by Royal Warrant to meet the requirements
of a legacy. He was the son of a small Yorkshire squire, and
throughout all his life he was faithful to the traditions of the

[1] [The Athenaeum.—Ed.]

95

squire class. He had no great intellectual qualities but he had the power of absorption. He could absorb a book on the opinions of a man. But there was no philosophy in his mental process. He was the prize-winning type. He won a scholarship to Eton and another from Eton to Oxford, where he became a Fellow of All Souls.[1]

But he soon forsook the academic life for a more active participation in public affairs. He was one of 'Milner's young men', that brilliant team that Milner gathered round him after the end of the Boer War, to restore order in the conquered territories. While Dawson was working under Milner he gave a significant indication of where his heart really lay, for he used to save up his money and his holidays to return to England for the fox-hunting.

In South Africa he left the public service to become editor of the *Johannesburg Star*, and also correspondent of the *Daily Telegraph*. But his rise to a position of influence and power came almost by accident. Before the first World War he had lunch in London with Lady Northcliffe and Miss Douglas-Pennant. There were Press Ladies even in those days, and through the influence of these ladies Dawson met Lord Northcliffe, who offered him immediate employment and afterwards made him editor of *The Times*.

Things ran smoothly for Dawson till the end of the first War. Dawson was a strong and deeply convinced Conservative but he was on friendly terms with Lloyd George and he found no difficulty or inconsistency in supporting his Coalition Government. But he had increasingly serious difficulties with Northcliffe over matters of policy, and shortly

[1] All Souls played a quite important part in Dawson's later life. When he was Editor of *The Times*, it was there that he used to meet Halifax (Halifax, Simon and Archbishop Lang were Fellows of All Souls) to discuss plans and policies. Halifax was as intimate a friend of Dawson's as Baldwin himself. Sir John Simon sometimes joined in these collegiate confabulations. The Archbishop of Canterbury often discussed public affairs with Dawson. As a result of these meetings, *The Times* became known in Oxford as the All Souls Parish Magazine.

after the end of the War he had to leave *The Times*.[1] He also had differences with Lloyd George and became his uncompromising enemy for the rest of his life.

While he was out of *The Times*—and while Lloyd George was still in office, Milner, the Colonial Secretary, asked Lloyd George to appoint Dawson Permanent Under Secretary for the Colonies. Lloyd George would not. In 1921, Philip Kerr offered Dawson, on behalf of Lloyd George, the editorship of the *Daily Chronicle*, but this time Dawson would not. He gave the excuse that he was too deeply engaged in his work for the Rhodes Trust, but his real reason for refusing was the fact that the *Daily Chronicle* was owned by the Lloyd George political fund. He wanted no more to do with Lloyd George.

His political friend and ally was now Stanley Baldwin. The two men had much in common, not only in political beliefs, but also in temperament and inclination. Each tried to imagine that he had the mind and habits of a country squire, though one was, in fact, a Fellow of All Souls and a journalist, and the other was a capitalist and a Company director. They belonged to the same world, even if it was a world of make-believe.

When Major Astor took over *The Times*, he restored Dawson to the editorial chair. Dawson was not too anxious to return to *The Times*. He considered that newspaper editorship was not a worthy place for him; for long he had aspired to be a Governor-General.[2] His return was very advantageous for Baldwin. Dawson supported him steadfastly and was equally steadfast in his opposition to Lloyd

[1] Dawson's friends explained his departure from *The Times* on the grounds of differences of policy between himself and Northcliffe. These differences undoubtedly existed, but the friends of Northcliffe had a different explanation. They said that Dawson had been heard speaking 'disloyally' of Northcliffe over the telephone to Lady Astor and had been promptly dismissed for that reason.

[2] When Chamberlain became Prime Minister, Dawson's name was included among those put forward for the Governor-Generalship of Canada. Canada turned it down.

George. *The Times* is not read by many, but it is read by those who form the opinion of the masses,[1] and any politician can count himself lucky who can rely on its support.

It was natural that Baldwin should call on Dawson when he was faced with the challenge of the King's intended marriage. The first consultation between the men took place towards the end of October, when Baldwin told Dawson the full story of his first interview with the King. Dawson immediately engaged himself heart and soul on the side of the Prime Minister against the King, and he made himself busy in the cause in ways that were not normal for a journalist.

Dawson had an 'informed source' in intimate contact with the King's affairs, who kept *The Times* office posted of developments through the assistant editor, Mr. Barrington-Ward. This informed source, referred to in the *History of The Times* as 'A', was Mr. Walter Monckton.[2]

Dawson also called on many public men in and out of Parliament. He consulted with Neville Chamberlain, Chancellor of the Exchequer, Mr. Mackenzie King, Prime Minister of Canada, who was in London at that time, Mr. Bruce of Australia, and many others.

The question of Press publicity worried Baldwin. He was not worried because publicity might be damaging to the King, but only because publicity might break out at a moment that was damaging to himself. He consulted Dawson on the right moment for informing the public and the right method of doing so. Dawson was entirely in sympathy with Baldwin, but he counselled caution and delay. The time was not yet ripe to strike.

On 11th November Dawson saw the Archbishop of Canterbury and learned his views on the Crisis. On the same day and the following day Dawson had further talks with

---

[1] *The Times* made a particular appeal to clergymen, who were offered special subscription rates.
[2] See *History of The Times*, Vol. 4, part II, p. 1027.

Baldwin on the problem of launching the Press attack.[1] The personal popularity of the King was their greatest difficulty. Premature publicity might damage Baldwin's influence with the King, and it might even discredit the whole cause of Government versus King if it came at an unfortunate moment. These consultations were held before the King had disclosed his intention of marrying Mrs. Simpson.

On 13th November, Major Hardinge asked to see Dawson and disclosed the contents of the letter which he proposed to send to the King. Dawson warmly approved it. He called the letter a 'courageous' document.[2]

The 16th November was the day on which the King first told Baldwin that he meant to marry Mrs. Simpson. On that day Dawson conferred with Mr. Gwynne of the *Morning Post* and he also saw Baldwin.

Talks with the Prime Minister after that were more or less continuous and increasingly intimate. On 26th November Baldwin consulted Dawson on the morganatic proposal and the reference to the Dominions. What he told Dawson on that day was not disclosed to the Cabinet till the day after.[3]

The question of Press publicity had now become delicate and anxious. Dawson had prepared a leader. News of this leader leaked out and it was believed that proofs were circulating in Fleet Street, as an earnest of what *The Times* would do if the King proved obdurate. When he heard on 28th November that I had been summoned home by the King Dawson considered printing the leader at once to forestall any action I might take, but he stayed his hand.[4]

That is to say, he made no open move, but he had been

[1] See *History of The Times*, Vol. 4, part II, p. 1029.

[2] *History of The Times*, Vol. 4, part II, p. 1030. What can be said of a Private Secretary who discussed his master's affairs with the editor of an opposition newspaper and even disclosed the contents of a letter of severe criticism that he meant to send to his employer? Bad. Worse still when the master is a King, and the servant a public official.

[3] See Baldwin's speech in the House of Commons, 10th December, 1936.

[4] See *History of The Times*, Vol. 4, part II, p. 1033.

conducting in *The Times* a campaign against the King, almost in secret code. The ordinary reader may well have been puzzled by the seeming pointlessness of some of the statements in *The Times* during this quiet period, but I knew very well their purpose. There was an article on the appointment of a new Governor-General of South Africa[1] which insisted that the King and the King's representatives should keep themselves free from public scandal. There was a surprising statement that the Commons were fundamentally a united body, and would soon prove themselves to be a Council of State, with one heart and one mind, if any emergency should arise, at home or abroad. On the very eve of the great Press outburst, *The Times* carried a most enthusiastic account of the warm reception given to the Duke and Duchess of York in Edinburgh, and the Duke was quite deliberately referred to as the Heir Presumptive. To anyone who could read the code, the message was clear. The King was causing scandal, he could count on support from no Party in Parliament, and there was a popular Heir Presumptive waiting in the wings.

[1] Sir Patrick Duncan was the man concerned. He must have been startled to read such a stern and quite unwarranted admonition in the columns of *The Times*.

XII

ON SUNDAY, 29th November, Dawson made the move which began open hostilities against the King. Mr. Arthur Mann, editor of the *Yorkshire Post*, was in London. Dawson asked him to come to *The Times* office, and there he told him the inner story of the Crisis of the King's affairs. Mr. Mann left Dawson convinced that Abdication was the inevitable and the only solution of the Crisis. When Bishop Blunt made his famous speech of 1st December, Mr. Mann wrote his almost equally famous leader. The initiative was his own but he acted on Dawson's information. Most provincial newspapers, including the *Manchester Guardian*, published similar leaders on 2nd December. That was the first public mention of the Crisis in the British Press, but the London newspapers said nothing openly till next day. *The Times* had carried a full report of Bishop Blunt's speech. But there was no comment. Nor was there any comment in the *Morning Post* or the *Daily Telegraph*. Dawson had seen both Mr. Gwynne of the *Morning Post* and Lord Camrose of the *Daily Telegraph*. He saw them both twice in one week. He ran his own system of Press consultation, confined, of course, to the papers supporting Baldwin.

He also continued to be in constant consultation with Baldwin. Twice in the night of 2nd December Baldwin telephoned Dawson about *The Times*'s attitude to Mrs. Simpson. He said that the King had 'instructed' him to see that there was no attack on Mrs. Simpson in *The Times*. Nothing could be better calculated to rouse the hostility of an editor than an 'instruction' from anybody as to what he should or should not print. Baldwin was aware of this fact. If he had really wished well to the King he would have refused to deliver such a damaging message. But he telephoned twice, and he was a man who seldom used the telephone. He was engaged in 'hotting up' Dawson against the King.

The 2nd December was the critical day for Baldwin, when he told the King that his morganatic proposal was rejected. Before he went to this interview, he spent an hour with Dawson, having no other purpose than to enjoy the comfort of Dawson's sympathy and support. On that same day, *The Times* allowed it to be known in Fleet Street that the morganatic proposal had been rejected by the Cabinet.

The 2nd December was a day of disaster for the King, shaking his confidence in himself and driving him forward to desperate conclusions. It was on this day that the reign of terror which Dawson and his assistants directed against the King reached a crescendo. Mr. Barrington-Ward, assistant editor, promised Sir Walter Monckton, known in *The Times* records as 'A', that despite His Majesty's apprehensions the paper did not intend to publish the 'full life' of Mrs. Simpson in the 'next issue'.[1]

It was said in Fleet Street that the 'full life' would carry photographs of two former husbands, her mother's boarding house and other illustrations.

A promise to refrain from publication for the 'next issue' was regarded as a cat-and-mouse game, and the King was the mouse. Torture.

The first *Times* leader which openly discussed the Crisis was published on Thursday, 3rd December, but it was not till next day, Friday, that *The Times* declared itself in uncompromising terms. That leader was well-timed, for there were

[1] *History of The Times*, Vol. 4, part II, p. 1036. *The Times* record points out here that a telephone call from me to the King on that Wednesday evening confirmed his fear of sensational disclosures in Thursday's Press. 'The Duke of Windsor', it declares, 'was then certain that *The Times*, under the fluent and pitiless pen of Geoffrey Dawson, would lead the attack' (ibid., footnote).

signs of hesitancy in the other papers hostile to the King. The stand of *The Times* rallied them all to the cause. In the same issue it also endeavoured to stir up trouble in the City by talk of a Stock Exchange panic.

On Saturday, 5th December, the King took the final and fatal step. He officially informed the Prime Minister that he would abdicate. This was, of course, known to Dawson who was closer to Baldwin than almost any of his Cabinet colleagues, but it did not persuade him to soften his propaganda against the King. On the contrary, he intensified it. It was not enough for him that the King should quit the Throne. He must also be so discredited that there would be no lingering remnants of loyalty in the breasts of his former subjects. For that reason Dawson became increasingly hostile and bitter after he knew that the issue was decided. He published one little piece of journalism which was innocent-seeming on the surface, but which carried a most wounding and malicious innuendo.[1] *The Times* has never explained or apologized for this act, but it remains as a stain on the memory of Geoffrey Dawson.

On Tuesday, 8th December, *The Times* made an open and totally unnecessary attack on Mrs. Simpson with reference to the morganatic proposal. 'The Constitution,' it declared, 'is to be amended in order that she may carry in solitary prominence the brand of unfitness for the Queen's throne.' The same issue carried a reference to the late King, George the Fifth, whose last days, it was said, were 'clouded by anxiety for the future'. This information came to Dawson from the Archbishop of Canterbury. In fact, the Archbishop

[1] When Lord Brownlow read it he sent for *The Times* correspondent at Cannes, who had been acting as his Press intermediary. He told him to draw his editor's attention to the matter—and then cut him off completely and for good. [Immediately under Mrs. Simpson's statement offering to withdraw, *The Times* printed this social item: 'Thelma Viscountess Furness arrived at Southampton in the liner *Queen Mary* yesterday from New York.' Lady Furness had been an intimate friend of Edward VIII's, when he was Prince of Wales.—Ed.]

103

had told Dawson that King George's end had been hastened by his anxiety over his son's 'infatuation', and Dawson came very close to repeating it in print.

In the heat of a critical controversy, these tactics would have been tough. But the issue was already decided, as Dawson well knew. He was acting the part of the 'character assassin', meaning that the King should not only lose his Throne, which he had already agreed to surrender, but should also lose his reputation and his claim on public respect.

If Dawson's campaign was ruthless and unscrupulous, it was also very successful. In the early days of the Crisis the letters coming to *The Times* reflected 'unquestioning loyalty' to the King.[1] By the end of the Crisis they were over-whelmingly against him. Dawson could feel that he had done his work well.

But his work was not finished even when the King had officially resigned the Throne and was preparing for exile. On 11th December, when the King was no longer King, Dawson printed a final leader on the Abdication. It professed to be an impartial summing-up of the King's character, but it was couched in such terms as might be expected from a magistrate speaking to an incorrigible criminal in the dock. Under the veneer of smooth language, it was a biting and blistering piece of invective. The high-light was the well-known tag from Tacitus to the effect that all would have thought Edward fit to rule if he had never ascended the Throne.

It was Dawson's parting and wanton word. That, with his attack on Mrs. Simpson and his allegation about the death of George the Fifth, remains the memorial of Geoffrey Dawson, twice editor of *The Times* and Fellow of All Souls.

[1] *History of The Times*, Vol. 4, part II, p. 1043.

XIII

FROM THE moment that the King telephoned me on Saturday, 5th December, to announce his intention to abdicate, I was completely cut off from all participation in his affairs.

From that day until the following Thursday, I lived as a mere spectator of the drama. Of all my associates in the fight for the King, not one got in touch with me to offer me any information as to what was going on behind the scenes. I could not bring myself to ask them for news. Depressed and disappointed as I was, I took to making plans for planting trees in the fields of Cherkley, my Surrey home.

On Monday, 7th December, I went to London to see Sir Samuel Hoare. He told me about the fate of the Bill to hasten the Simpson divorce which Baldwin had promised the King. After that, I was alone in Cherkley.

I made only one attempt to learn what was happening, and that attempt was made on the basis of a long and intimate friendship. I telephoned Lord Brownlow, who was in Cannes, but I got no satisfaction. Lord Brownlow simply dodged my request for news.[1]

I could not do anything even with my newspapers. They were struggling to uphold the reputation of the King, which was now being violently assailed by the 'Baldwin' Press, but I could take no hand in the issue and I could do nothing to shape the policy of the *Express* and *Standard*, because I had the secret knowledge that Abdication had already been decided on.

[1] He explained afterwards that his telephone was tapped.

105

On Tuesday morning, 8th December, the Press published a statement from Mrs. Simpson:

'Mrs. Simpson throughout the last few weeks has invariably wished to avoid any action or proposal which would hurt or damage the King or the Throne.

'Today her attitude is unchanged, and she is willing, if such action would solve the problem, to withdraw forthwith from a situation that has been rendered unhappy and untenable.'

It was a strange and puzzling declaration. Why did Mrs. Simpson make this statement at a time when she knew that the King had abdicated? Curious!

The *Daily Express* took too much notice of the statement and made a big story of it. That was my fault. I would not give the newspaper any direction. Though I knew that the statement did not mean a thing.[1] *The Times* and other Baldwin newspapers took very little notice of Mrs. Simpson's disclaimer.

It is difficult to describe the loneliness that descended on me at Cherkley. I had been plunged into the middle of a momentous and enthralling crisis, and for days I had lived in a tornado of excitement and activity. I was never at rest, either by night or by day. One emergency followed another. There were almost incessant telephone calls by day and night, and confidential meetings with the King, with a constant demand for hurried but vital decisions.

Now there was silence, total and unbroken. The tornado was still raging but it had passed me by. The abrupt change from the extreme of activity in the very heart of affairs to complete inactivity and isolation had a physical reaction. My toothache returned.

[1] Lord Brownlow drew up this statement, but he did not believe it would have any effect. When he gave it to the Press at Cannes he refused to say a single word in addition to the written message. He had many telephone calls from reporters asking for enlightenment but he refused to make comment.

I had been suffering from toothache when I was first brought into the affair, but the engrossing nature of the struggle and the immense demands it made, both physical and mental, had banished 'the Hell of all diseases' from my mind. Now it came back to be the sole and unwelcome companion of my solitude.

At last I paid my return visit to the dentist, Mr. Campbell. By that time, the drama was over. Baldwin had already spoken and the King was preparing to speak for the first and last time. While I was in the dentist's chair, the assistant came in to say that I was being asked to receive a telephone call from Buckingham Palace. I was confused and uncertain when I heard this summons, and I replied 'Buckingham Palace—no more'. The fight had been lost and the most stubborn enemy of our plan for a United British Empire had scored his greatest triumph.[1] Mr. Campbell took note of my hesitancy, and he laid his instruments down. He was surprised that a call from the Palace on that day of all days should not have brought me instantly to my feet, in haste to answer. I was in no hurry, but I shuffled to the telephone and there had a brief exchange of good wishes. To a brave spirit even more tormented than I was depressed I spoke in cheerful terms. Then back to the dentist's chair.

That night the late King motored to Portsmouth to board the destroyer *Fury*, and put out to sea. He went into exile from which he has not yet returned. But he was not without hope and expectation. 'Journeys end in lovers' meetings', and he was so much nearer to the desire of his heart.

The ex-King had spent his time on the journey across the

---

[1] Baldwin remained in power till after the Coronation of King George the Sixth. He had a tremendous reception when he drove in the Coronation procession, perhaps greater than the King himself. A fortnight afterwards he retired into private life. But his last years were hag-ridden by self-reproach at the thought of all that he had left undone for the defence of Britain. He would talk about nothing else. Whatever subject of conversation was raised by his friends, Baldwin soon returned to his endless self-justification which was, in fact, self-condemnation.

Channel in sending wireless messages of farewell and thanks and good wishes to his friends and supporters in England. He was still engaged on this task when *Fury* reached territorial waters and he was told that the wireless could no longer be used. The ex-King ordered the ship back to sea until he had finished his task. Then *Fury* made port. The man who had been King stepped ashore at Boulogne. No cheering multitudes, no waving flags, no military music for the fallen Monarch. He was just a noted traveller journeying to a foreign city.[1]

I also went away, resuming the journey to New York that had been so abruptly ended by the call from the King. In a few days I stood on the very pier from which I had boarded ship and turned back in response to the King's message.

One day President Roosevelt asked me to go to Washington to see him. When I got there the President took a short respite from affairs of State to examine and re-examine me on every detail of the royal tragedy. He could not understand it. He quoted the old saying that no man should ever resign, but should wait to be sacked. I tried to explain to the President that the King had in the end left himself no option but to abdicate. He had yielded so often to the politicians in the course of the negotiations that he had lost five separate battles. In the final stages of his crisis there was a point of no return. There were suicidal errors of judgement, from which there could be no hope of recovery.

I felt that the President was not entirely convinced by my explanation, but I could not at the time make myself any clearer than I did. But, many years afterwards I was told of

[1] The King made his last public appearance on Armistice Day 1936 amid scenes of splendid pageantry with his veterans and comrades of the Great War. He entered the Royal Box at the Albert Hall accompanied by the Earl of Munster, Lord in Waiting, and was received with unbounded enthusiasm. Six-fold roars of cheers rang out and after the Anthem the cheering was renewed. He was indeed a popular hero. On his return to Buckingham Palace, he told his attending Ministers that he was encouraged by his reception to face the crisis over his intentions to marry Mrs. Simpson. He believed he could pull it off.

a remark by the abdicated King which gave the clue to the whole tragedy in a single sentence.

When he disembarked from *Fury* at Boulogne, and bade farewell to the friends who had come with him, he turned to one of them and said, 'I always thought I could get away with the morganatic marriage.'

If I had known of this parting conversation when I talked with President Roosevelt I could have given him in the words of a King the answer to the question—Why? 'I always thought I could get away with the morganatic marriage.'

Years after the events described in this narrative, Churchill was painting a scene at my villa on the French Riviera. The conversation turned hither and thither on many political struggles in the early days when we sat on opposite sides of the House.

Churchill said one or other had certainly been right or wrong, as we had always differed. Except once, I said, mentioning the Abdication.

'Perhaps we were both wrong that time,' was his reply.

Appendix A

UNTIL THE early years of the twentieth century, appearance in a divorce case carried heavy penalties in many directions. It was nearly always fatal to a political career, and was equally fatal in the social circles that took their tone from the Court. The Court upheld the Anglican principle that marriage could be dissolved only by death. Those who denied that principle by seeking the relief that the Civil Law allowed were no longer received by the Royal Family.

With a few exceptions, such as Sir Charles Dilke,[1] the Member of Parliament who had gone through the divorce court could consider his political career as at a close. The last man to suffer from this convention was Eliot Crawshay Williams, Lloyd George's Parliamentary Private Secretary. I sat with him in the Commons and knew him well. In 1913, he was cited as co-respondent by a fellow Liberal Member, and he resigned from his minor post in the Government and vacated his seat in Parliament. He resigned unwillingly and wrote to his constituents saying, 'It is perhaps a pity that circumstances which do nothing to impair political capacity should be able to interfere with political activity.'

He made a mistake. For there was no Election until 1918 and by that time the barrier against divorced men in Parliament was falling. It still occasionally happened that a divorced man might not seek re-election. But Members no longer resigned their seats because they had been divorced.

The barrier still blocked a man from becoming a Minister of the Crown until it was broken down by that remarkable character, Colonel Josiah Wedgwood. His wife was granted a divorce

[1] [Though Dilke gave up his seat at Chelsea and forfeited his chance of a place in the Cabinet, he was subsequently returned for the Forest of Dean and remained a Member of Parliament until his death.—Ed.]

decree on the grounds of desertion and adultery. As there were seven children of the marriage the case created a painful impression. On the day when the newspapers told the story of the case, Wedgwood spoke six times in the Commons, in total silence.

But Wedgwood took an extraordinary step to justify himself. He wrote to a newspaper in his constituency and explained that the desertion was a mere formality. He and his wife had lived apart for many years. To facilitate the divorce which she wanted, Wedgwood had first staged a technical 'desertion' and then provided 'evidence' of adultery, though no adultery had taken place. The device of pretending adultery was common enough, but it was distinctly unusual to make a public declaration that the offence had not, in fact, been committed.

In spite of his divorce and his subsequent outburst, Wedgwood became a Cabinet Minister in the first Labour Government, a Privy Councillor, and, later, a Peer. Thereafter many men appointed to Cabinet rank have been through the divorce court.

Until the first World War, divorce was also nearly always a barrier against the granting of Royal Honours. George the Fifth, a man of simple piety, was anxious to maintain that barrier. It was broken for the first time, so far as I know, by Lloyd George. When he was Chancellor of the Exchequer, he succeeded in securing a knighthood for George Riddell, the newspaper proprietor, who had been divorced. Riddell was made a baronet when he was Prime Minister.

Lloyd George may have had some personal sympathy with the endeavour to break down the divorce barrier, for his own career had been nearly ruined by a divorce action in 1897. He was cited as a co-respondent and it was alleged that he had committed adultery with a woman on February 4th of that year. Fortunately, he was able to establish his innocence by showing that he had been in the House of Commons until one o'clock in the morning on February 5th. The Division List was absolute proof of his innocence, but his enemies had been rubbing their hands in the belief that his appearance in a divorce action would put a summary end to his career.

When Lloyd George was Prime Minister and when he was about to go to the country, he had to meet the formidable opposition of Northcliffe who controlled both *The Times* and the

111

Daily Mail. Northcliffe was running a strong campaign against Lloyd George, who accordingly, sought to rally Press support for himself and his Coalition candidates. He could rely on George Riddell who was his most intimate friend, and, through me, he could also rely on the *Express.* But he wanted more support, and at Lloyd George's request I arranged a meeting for him with Lord Rothermere and Edward Hulton. These men pledged their support at the Election of 1918 and fully honoured their pledge.

After the Election, Lloyd George recommended Riddell, Hulton and Rothermere for Honours. Rothermere, then a Baron, was made a Viscount forthwith. He had never been in the divorce court. Court circles objected to Riddell, but his peerage was granted in 1920 after strong pressure.

There was even more stubborn resistance to the baronetcy proposed for Edward Hulton, who had also been divorced, and it was not until 1921 that it was granted, after much controversy between Buckingham Palace and Downing Street.

Thus, in the early Twenties the divorce barrier had been breached. Divorce was no longer a complete barrier to political preferment and Royal Honours were being given to divorced persons. There was also a breach, slowly widening, in the social sphere. There had previously been a hard and fast rule that nobody who had been through the divorce court could be received in presentation at Court or could be granted an entry to the coveted Royal Enclosure at Ascot. A few exceptions began to be made, first for innocent divorced persons and later for guilty persons. There was no clear reason why some should be excepted and others not, except that some were richer and more influential than others. One lady of high position who was greatly admired by her friends secured a presentation at Court, though she had been through the divorce court. Within a month the *London Gazette* announced that the presentation had been cancelled. The woman's name was given. It is difficult to conceive of a more cruel and more outrageous insult to a lady.

Less publicly humiliating but even more surprising was the action taken against Sir Basil Blackett. Sir Basil Blackett, C.B., K.C.B., K.C.S.I., was an eminent Civil Servant. He became a Director of the Bank of England and of Cable and Wireless and other important companies. His first marriage was dissolved, and he re-married in 1920. In 1922, he received an invitation to a Royal Garden Party, but, because of the divorce proceedings that invitation was withdrawn, in spite of his high official standing and his great public services. At the time when his invitation was withdrawn he was still a Civil Servant and one of the most valuable of all the officers of the Crown. His skill, knowledge and devotion continued to be used though, socially, he was treated as an outcast.

Nevertheless, the divorce barrier was breaking down all round and it looked as if it might be swept away altogether. In 1936, the year of the Abdication, there were thirteen Members of the Commons who had been through the divorce court. It is a pity that only one of those spoke up for the King.

In the years following the Abdication divorce has ceased to be a barrier except in Court circles. The Anglican boycott of divorced persons is drawing to a close. The taboo has ceased to have any effect at all in Society. In 1938, a divorced man became a Judge of the High Court, and today there are three eminent Judges who have been through the divorce court. Several holders of the highest ranks in the fighting Services have also been before the divorce courts. The granting of Honours to divorced persons is now a commonplace. In 1949, the Order of Merit, which is by far the rarest of intellectual distinctions, was conferred on Bertrand Russell who had twice been divorced as the guilty party.

In 1951 Mr. Churchill selected three members of his Cabinet who have been named as respondents or co-respondents in successful divorce cases. Since then, we have had a Prime Minister, Sir Anthony Eden, who had divorced his wife and married again.

Some inconsistencies still prevail. For example, when Lloyd George was Prime Minister, the Duke of Marlborough was called upon to resign the Lord Lieutenancy of Oxfordshire. He had been divorced and re-married and had been refused Communion in the Church of England. Lord Birkenhead went to Oxford on behalf of the Government to urge the Duke to resign. The Duke flatly and finally refused and dared the Government to dismiss him. The Government did not dismiss him.

But more than twenty years afterwards, when the divorce

113

barrier was almost totally swept away, the Duke of Sutherland was dismissed. He had married a divorced lady and when called upon to resign he refused. He was then dismissed. And the reprobation of the Court did not cease with his dismissal. The Duke of Sutherland was Senior Vice-President of the Highland Show. He had subscribed largely to the funds and had presented a silver cup. Yet, when the Show was held at Inverness he was informed that his own name and that of his Duchess had been struck off the list of those invited to lunch with the King and Queen. He was told that this was not done voluntarily by the Committee of the Show, but on instructions from higher authority.

At the present time the Governor of one of our Colonies has been through the divorce court as a co-respondent. Yet, he is the official representative of His Majesty. I agree that his appointment in face of his divorce was proper and I deeply regret that a similar appointment was refused, on grounds of divorce, to a war-time Commander with a brilliant record of service to the nation.

Thus, there are still illogical and inconsistent survivals of the old bar, but they are exceptions. In general, it may be said that the barrier against divorced persons has been almost completely swept away, and before long we may expect that not a trace of the ancient prejudice will remain.

It was unfortunate that Mrs. Simpson's divorce occurred in the middle of the movement for freedom from ecclesiastical intolerance. It was doubly unfortunate that it occurred at a time when the Church of England was making a great effort to re-assert its principles and re-establish its position. The Church's campaign was a forlorn hope, but it was conducted with vigour, and Mrs. Simpson fell victim to the fury of a last counter-attack. It made no difference in the eyes of the Church that she was aggrieved and innocent in both the divorce cases in which she had been implicated.

Appendix B

MR. BALDWIN AS COMPANY DIRECTOR

MR. BALDWIN'S career before taking Government office was
mainly that of a company director. At one time or another he
held directorships in the following concerns:

Aldridge Colliery Company Ltd.
Alexandra (Newport & South Wales) Docks & Railway Com-
pany.
Baldwins Ltd.
Gloucester Railway Carriage & Wagon Company Ltd.
Grand Trunk Pacific Railway Company.
Grand Trunk Railway Company of Canada.
Great Western Railway Company.
Legeh Concessions Syndicate Ltd.
Metropolitan Bank (of England & Wales) Ltd.
Port Talbot Steel Company Ltd.
South Wales Mineral Railway Company.
United Tube Corporation Ltd.
West London Extension Railway Company.

Appendix C

NARRATIVE OF MR. THEODORE GODDARD, SOLICITOR OF MRS. SIMPSON

The following statement was written in July 1951 and authorized for publication by a letter from Goddard to Lord Beaverbrook dated 23rd July, 1951.

IN THE year 1936 I was consulted by Mrs. Wallis Simpson (now the Duchess of Windsor) and instructed to take proceedings for divorce against her husband, Mr. Simpson.

The case was a perfectly straightforward one and the evidence complete and it was not defended.

The witnesses to prove the case were at Maidenhead, where the adultery had taken place and for the convenience of witnesses I endeavoured to get the case tried at the following Reading Assize.

It so happened that at that Assize they were not taking Divorce cases. Mrs. Simpson was anxious to get the case through as soon as possible and so I set the case down for hearing at the next convenient Assize, namely Ipswich and my recollection is that it came on for trial there as Undefended case before Mr. Justice Hawke.

In accordance with the instructions of Mrs. Simpson, I retained Sir Norman Birkett, K.C. (then Mr. Birkett, K.C.) to lead Mr. Walter Frampton, who was the Junior in the case. This meant taking Sir Norman off his regular Circuit and required the usual special fee to be paid to him. The object in briefing Sir Norman Birkett and taking him off his own Assize was to prevent any suggestion that Mrs. Simpson was trying to hush up the case—indeed she had no desire to do this—and as I advised

116

her at the time, as I had briefed Sir Norman Birkett, the case would in due course get all publicity.

*

The next incident in the matter was about ten days before the case was due to come on, when Lord Beaverbrook rang me up and told me his newspaper the *Evening Standard*, had got the information and he proposed to publish a statement the following day in the *Evening Standard* that the case was coming on.

I immediately went and saw Lord Beaverbrook and I told him that while there was not the slightest objection to all publicity being given to the report of the actual proceedings, I thought it was most undesirable that there should be any comment or press statement beforehand.

I was with Lord Beaverbrook for some two hours that night at Cherkley and left him on the understanding that he would think it over and would let me know.

The following morning in company with Sir Walter Monckton K.C. and Mr. Allen I went to Buckingham Palace and saw the King. I told the King exactly what had happened at my interview with Lord Beaverbrook and I suggested that he might feel inclined to ring up Lord Beaverbrook at Cherkley and reiterate what I had said to him and make it clear that there was no desire whatever to stop any report of the proceedings but merely to stop press announcements beforehand. Lord Beaverbrook agreed and later in the day he told me that other papers had the information.

That evening in company with Sir Walter Monckton and Mr. Allen, I telephoned from my private house in Connaught Square all the leading newspaper proprietors in the country. It took us some three hours to do this. Fortunately with the successful result that no papers published in advance any statement about the case.

The case was duly tried at Ipswich and a decree *nisi* was made upon evidence which was unquestionable.

About this time I received a message from Sir Warren Fisher, who was then Head of the Treasury, that he would very much like to see me and I saw him on the Saturday afternoon. Sir Warren's trouble was that he had got grounds for believing the

King meant to marry Mrs. Simpson and was there anything I could do to prevent it. I explained to Sir Warren that that was not my function, so far as I was concerned it was merely a straightforward Undefended divorce case and it was no part of my duty to advise Mrs. Simpson on the question of any future marriage at all. Sir Warren was very friendly and very understanding. He called in several of his colleagues, Sir Horace Wilson, Lord Vansittart and one or two others and they eventually all agreed with my view about the matter, except Sir Horace Wilson but I emphasized to Sir Horace very definitely my intentions in the matter and the interview came to an end.

I have on many occasions since then discussed the matter with Sir Warren and he and I became great friends.

The next incident that I remember (and it would be some weeks later) Sir Horace Wilson, who was acting as Head of the Treasury in the absence of Sir Warren Fisher, who was away owing to illness, asked me to come and see him, which I did.

At this time, Mrs. Simpson was in the South of France and he told me that he thought Mr. Baldwin, who was then Prime Minister, would like me to see Mrs. Simpson to ascertain from her her real intentions.

On the following Monday (i.e. the Monday before the abdication) I was summoned to The Fort with Sir Walter Monckton and Mr. Allen and I had a long private interview with the King when the matter was very frankly discussed. I gathered that the King knew that I had been asked to see Mrs. Simpson in the South of France and that it was my intention to carry out that request.

That evening I went to Downing Street and saw Lord Baldwin. He had in his hand a statement which had been issued to the Press on behalf of Mrs. Simpson, which I had not seen before, dealing generally with the position but not stating one way or the other what her intentions were. This statement I gathered had been issued on her behalf when she was in the South of France because of Press comment.

Mr. Baldwin, as he then was, showed me the statement and asked me what I knew about it. I told him I knew nothing. I said I gathered that he wanted me to see Mrs. Simpson and that if that was so I would certainly go. He asked me to do this.

I flew that night to the South of France but owing to bad weather conditions we did not get there until late on Tuesday night. I travelled in a small Government plane. One of the engines broke down.

As soon as I did get to the South of France, I telephoned to Mrs. Simpson. It was then 2 o'clock in the morning. I arranged to see her about 9 o'clock the following morning, which I did.

I had a long talk with her. I told her so far as I knew it what I gathered was the feeling in this country and I asked her whether it was wise for her to contemplate a marriage with the King. After a long talk she definitely said she was quite prepared to give him up[1] but she did say that wherever she went the King would follow her. As a result both she and I had a long telephone conversation with the King, during which the King indicated his definite intention of marrying Mrs. Simpson and of abdicating the throne. The call was a very bad one, there were continual interruptions.

I returned to England that night. There was no plane to bring me so I travelled by train to Paris, arriving there at 7 o'clock in the morning. I was there met by the First or Second Secretary to the Embassy and he drove me to Le Bourget where a Government plane was waiting for me. He told me that he had been instructed by Downing Street to obtain from me the result of my interview with Mrs. Simpson and that he was going to telephone it through. The Prime Minister was about to speak in the House of Commons that afternoon and wanted to have this information before he spoke. Having satisfied myself that the gentleman was the Secretary to the Embassy I reported to him the result of my interviews.

I then left for London. I was met at the Airport and driven straight to Downing Street. I got there about 12.30. I immediately saw Sir Horace Wilson, who had already had the report I had given to the Secretary to the Embassy in Paris and I could not help but gather from my conversation with him that he already knew all about it and seemed to know something of our conversations with the King.

It is difficult after all these years to be precise and absolutely

[1] Mr. Goddard asked whether in the circumstances it was wise to continue with the divorce proceedings and to obtain the decree absolute.

accurate in one's recollection, although my recollection is fairly clear and two points are outstanding:

1. Mrs. Simpson was prepared to give up the King.
2. That the King was definite in his decision that he would not give her up: that he intended to abdicate and eventually marry her.

Appendix D

(i)

Lord Beaverbrook to J. M. Patterson, 23rd January, 1936.

... The new reign gives us a new outlook in public life. For, of course, the King has little power but great influence. He can set a tone in the country.

It is difficult to forecast what the effect will be. I think that the nearest approach to a survey of future possibilities is that outlined by A. J. Cummings in the *News Chronicle.*

He takes the view that the new King is dominated by an interest in the ex-servicemen, regarding as his comrades those who fought in the war. This may be expected to give him a special interest in social improvements.

He will be quite different from his Father. He is casual in manner, unconventional and independent-minded. He has few friends among the politicians. All these are qualities which may turn out well or badly. And, in considering how he will use them, it must be remembered that he is by no means stupid.

Then Cummings adds some words of warning and advice. The King must leave behind him the care-free and unconventional side of his life. His life does not belong to himself, his friends, or the ex-servicemen. It belongs to the Nation.

And he must not cause anxiety to his Ministers by impatience or ill-temper.

In all the foregoing, I am giving you the opinion of Cummings, a very able journalist writing for a Liberal newspaper. Plainly, there are aspects of character against which Cummings gives friendly warning. But the final impression is one of optimism.

This is the impression most people have formed.

. . . .

121

Lord Beaverbrook to Roy W. Howard, 8th December, 1936.

. . . .

Just at the moment we, in Britain, cannot see so far off as Asia. Indeed, we are hardly giving any attention to Europe. The Spanish War is tucked away into the inside pages of the newspapers.

It looks as if Europe could get on without us, after all. And perhaps, now that we have dropped Europe, we shall not pick it up again.

We have all become King's men or Cabinet men. It is as if the whole country had slipped back into the seventeenth century again.

. . . .

The opposition to the King's project of marriage to Mrs. Simpson is essentially religious in character. He is lay head of the Church of England, and the chief priests and the Sanhedrin say, in effect, that he may live in sin with her, but must not marry a woman who has been married twice before.

Now, of course everybody does not take that view. The divorced and the free thinkers, for example, might be expected to line up on the King's side. But the trouble about these two elements is this—The divorced are all hard at work trying to become respectable. And the free thinkers don't care much about the monarchy anyway.

The Fascists and the Communists, those tiny factions, give embarrassing support to the King. They are trying to convert the dispute into a conflict of King versus Parliament. They will not have any success.

But there is a large body of opinion in the country—respectable opinion—which believes that this King has built up for himself a position with the people, that gives strength and stability to the whole political structure. This sort of opinion does not much like the marriage with Mrs. Simpson, but it is willing to make concessions in order to keep the King.

By the time you get this, the whole issue may be settled. I hope it is, because there are other things to attend to.

Lord Beaverbrook

LORD BEAVERBROOK was born William Maxwell Aitken in 1879 in Maple, Ontario, Canada. He was one of ten children of a Presbyterian minister. He grew up in New Brunswick, where he briefly studied law, sold insurance, ran a bowling alley, and worked in the meat business. By the age of thirty he had amassed a fortune as a wizard in corporate finance by promoting industrial mergers in steel, electric power, cement, and other industries. He settled in England in 1910 and successfully ran for Parliament as a Conservative. Six years later he was elevated to the House of Lords as the first Baron Beaverbrook. That year he bought control of the *Daily Express,* which, under his supervision, grew from a circulation of 229,000 to over four million. He later acquired the *Sunday Express, London Evening Standard,* and *Glasgow Evening Citizen.*

However, Lord Beaverbrook's main interests were political. During World War II he was Minister of Aircraft Production under Sir Winston Churchill, who called him "my oldest and closest friend." His books include *Politicians and the Press* (1925), *Politicians and the War* (1928), *Men and Power* (1954), *Friends* (1959), *The Divine Propagandist* (1962), and *The Decline and Fall of Lloyd George* (1963).

Lord Beaverbrook died in 1964.